The Church under the Penal Code

JOHN BRADY & PATRICK J. CORISH

Irish Exiles in Catholic Europe

CATHALDUS GIBLIN O.F.M.

A History of Irish Catholicism

General Editor · Patrick J. Corish

A HISTORY OF IRISH CATHOLICISM

VOLUME IV

2

The Church under the Penal Code

John Brady and Patrick J. Corish

3

Irish Exiles in Catholic Europe

Cathaldus Giblin, O.F.M.

GILL AND MACMILLAN

First published 1971

Gill and Macmillan Limited
2 Belvedere Place
Dublin 1
and in London through association with
Macmillan and Co. Ltd.

282.H15

H673

V.4

pt 2 3

BX 1503
H55
Vol. 4
no. 2/3

COVER DESIGNED BY DES FITZGERALD

7171   0516   4

Printed in the Republic of Ireland by Cahill and Co. Limited,
Parkgate Street, Dublin 8.

BIBLIOGRAPHICAL ABBREVIATIONS

Bibliographical abbreviations follow in general the list given in *Irish Historical Studies,* Supplement I (January 1968). A bibliography, together with a full list of abbreviations, will be published with the completion of the text of the volume. The following are noted for the convenience of readers of this fascicule.

Manuscripts and Archives

A.P.F.	Archivio della S. Congregazione de Propaganda Fide
C.P.	Congregazioni particolari
S.C., Irlanda	Scritture riferite nei congressi, Irlanda
A.V.	Archivio Vaticano
Sec. Brevium	Secretariat of Briefs
Nunz.	Nunziatura

Printed Books

B.M. cat. Ir. MSS	*Catalogue of Irish Manuscripts in the British Museum,* 2 vols., London 1926.
Ball, *Judges*	F. E. Ball, *The judges in Ireland, 1221-1921,* 2 vols., London 1926.
Begley, *Limerick*	J. Begley, *The diocese of Limerick from 1691 to the present time,* Dublin 1938.
Bellesheim, *Geschichte*	A. Bellesheim, *Geschichte der katholischen Kirche in Irland,* 3 vols., Mainz 1890-91.
Brady, *Eighteenth-century press*	J. Brady, *Catholics and Catholicism in the eighteenth-century press,* Maynooth 1965.
Burke, *Hib. Dom.*	T. de Burgo, *Hibernia Dominicana,* Cologne 1772; *Supplementum,* Cologne 1776.
Burke, *Penal times*	W. P. Burke, *The Irish priests in the penal times, 1660-1760,* Waterford 1914, reprinted Shannon 1969.
Carrigan, *Ossory*	W. Carrigan, *The history and antiquities of the Diocese of Ossory,* 4 vols., Dublin 1905.
Cogan, *Meath*	A. Cogan, *The ecclesiastical history of the diocese of Meath,* 3 vols., Dublin 1867-74.
Comerford, *Kildare* and *Leighlin*	D. Comerford, *Collections relating to the dioceses of Kildare and Leighlin,* 3 vols., Dublin 1883-86.

Commons' jn. Ireland	*Journals of the House of Commons of the kingdom of Ireland*, Dublin 1753 ff.
D.N.B.	*Dictionary of national biography*, 66 vols., London 1885-1901.
Donnelly, *Dublin parishes*	N. Donnelly, *A short history of some Dublin parishes*, Dublin 1904.
H.M.C.	Historical Manuscripts Commission.
Hayes, *Biographical dictionary*	R. Hayes, *Biographical dictionary of Irishmen in France*, Dublin 1949.
Healy, *Maynooth college*	J. Healy, *Maynooth college: its centenary history*, Dublin 1895.
Lecky, *Ire.*	W. E. H. Lecky, *History of Ireland in the eighteenth century*, 5 vols., London 1892.
Lords' jn. Ire.	*Journal of the House of Lords of Ireland*, Dublin 1799-1800.
Moran, *Spicil. Ossor.*	P. F. Moran, *Spicilegium Ossoriense*, 3 vols., Dublin 1874-84.
O'Connell, *Kilmore*	P. O'Connell, *The diocese of Kilmore, its history and antiquities*, Dublin 1937.
O'Laverty, *Down and Connor*	J. O'Laverty, *An historical account of the diocese of Down and Connor*, 5 vols., Dublin 1878-95.
Renehan, *Collections*	L. F. Renehan, *Collections on Irish church history* (ed. D. McCarthy), 2 vols., Dublin 1861, 1874.
Ritzler-Sefrin, *Hierarchia Catholica*	R. Ritzler and P. Sefrin, *Hierarchia Catholica medii et recentioris aevi*, V (1667-1730), Padua 1942; VI (1730-99), Padua 1948.
Ware, *Writers*	J. Ware, *The writers of Ireland* (in vol. II of *The works of Sir James Ware*, revised and ed. W. Harris), Dublin 1746.

Periodicals

Anal. Hib.	*Analecta Hibernica*, Dublin 1930—.
Archiv. Hib.	*Archivium Hibernicum*, Maynooth 1912—.
Coll. Hib.	*Collectanea Hibernica*, Dublin 1958—.
I.E.R.	*Irish Ecclesiastical Record*, Dublin 1864-1968.
I.H.S.	*Irish Historical Studies*, Dublin 1938—.
Ossory Arch. Soc. Trans.	*Transactions of the Ossory Archaeological Society*, Kilkenny 1874-83.
Rep. Novum	*Reportorium Novum*, Dublin 1955—.
Waterford Arch. Soc. Jn.	*Journal of the Waterford and south-east of Ireland Archaeological Society*, Waterford 1894-1920.

II

THE CHURCH UNDER THE PENAL CODE

*John Brady and Patrick J. Corish**

*John Brady and Patrick J. Corish**

PERMISSION TO EXIST

PROPERTY and religion lie at the root of the three great upheavels, the Ulster plantation, the Cromwellian confiscation, and the Williamite settlement, which fashioned the pattern of eighteenth-century Ireland. It was more than a coincidence that in each case most of the victims of confiscation were Catholics and the beneficiaries Protestants; but it would be over-simplification to attribute the change to religion alone. A recent study puts the Catholic ownership of land in 1641 at 59 per cent, in 1688 at 22 per cent, and in 1703 at 14 per cent.[1] Reliable statistics of the religious affiliations of the population are less easy to find, but figures claimed to be based on the hearth-money returns represent the population in 1731 as 1,309,768 Catholics and 700,456 Protestants, and in 1766 as 1,671,478 Catholics and 682,815 Protestants.[2]

The new proprietors were a fragment of the population and from them was drawn the bulk of the legislators. When they spoke, as they frequently did, of 'safeguarding the Protestant interest' they had in mind the perpetuation of

---

*When Father John Brady died on 30 September 1963 he had completed little more than the first two sections of this chapter. In writing the remainder, I have used some rough drafts he had made and have had access to his notebooks, the fruit of a lifetime's exploration of the byways of eighteenth-century catholicism. *Requiescat in pace*. P.J.C.

---

1. Simms, *The Williamite confiscation in Ireland, 1690-1703*, 195.

2. Brady, *Eighteenth-century press*, 226-7. Modern research indicates all such figures to be underestimates, but the proportions are probably right.

A

their own new property and privileges and the reduction of their Catholic neighbours to a condition of permanent servitude. Society in eighteenth-century Ireland was organized on the assumption that Catholics, who formed the majority of the population, were an inferior class, unworthy of trust and unfit for civil rights. This notion, the product of more than a century of misrepresentation in which no crime was too heinous to attribute to Papists, as they were contemptuously called, was widely and tenaciously held by Protestants who used it to justify enacting and retaining an elaborate code of laws designed to constrict and control 'Popery' rather than destroy it.

The nature of these laws is analysed elsewhere. Under the slogan of 'safeguarding the Protestant interest' the legislators, a small minority, made the perpetuation of property, power and privilege, which had been theirs since the defeat of James II, their main objective rather than the propagation of protestantism. They thought of catholicism as a dangerous, untrustworthy political system rather than as a religion. Hence the nature of the legislation directed against it and the speed with which it was enforced in times of political insecurity such as in 1715. Hence the willingness of the minority to close their eyes at other times to infringements if Catholics were content to subsist as a subject people, giving no cause for fear or offence to the master race. 'It was intended,' says Lecky, 'to make them poor and to keep them poor, to crush in them every germ of enterprise, to degrade them into a servile caste who could never hope to rise to the level of their oppressors.' In this atmosphere of suspicion, contempt and inferiority Catholics subsisted for the greater part of the century.

Except in times of political unrest the executive found it prudent to turn a blind eye to Catholics openly practising their religion when this did not seem to it to endanger 'the Protestant interest' and when Catholics were content to remain subject to their masters. When in 1759 the Irish chancellor, Lord Bowes, declared that the laws of Ireland did not presume a Roman Catholic to exist, nor could one breathe there without the connivance of the government,[3] he had before him over sixty years of legislation enacted with the deliberate intention of reducing the majority to a condition of political impotence, of buttressing a minority in power and privilege. The chancellor's statement was accepted without question by the Irish judicial bench, which was unfavourable to any change in the laws. It made clear what the legal position was and implied that the existence of Irish Catholics was due to the non-enforcement of these laws, a fact that Catholics were expected to remember with gratitude and contentment. In 1745 the Protestant archbishop of Tuam, in common with the rest of the hierarchy, was thoroughly alarmed by the Jacobite rising in England and Scotland and in a pastoral letter to his flock advised them to reason with their Catholic neighbours:

> Do they not through his majesty's clemency, enjoy the free exercise of their religion, even at this very conjuncture, when they might expect to be restrained? Do they not resort as publicly in great numbers to their Mass-houses, without the least molestation, as Protestants do to their churches? Is not the priest in every parish well known to the Protestant gentlemen, and tho' he be liable to prosecution, yet does any one lay hold of him, or disturb him so long as he behaves himself orderly and decently as becomes his character? Now, if these are all undeniable facts, what can any modest and reasonable Papist desire more, and how can he be aggrieved?[4]

The traditional picture of the penal days is somewhat distorted inasmuch as it emphasizes the difficulties under which Catholics worshipped rather than the social and economic difficulties under which they lived. The latter were the more widespread and the more lasting, because the penal code appealed more to greed and ambition than to bigotry,

3. Ball, *Judges,* II, 152.
4. Brady, *Eighteenth-century press,* 70-71.

and fewer Catholics fell away from fear than from material motives.

The legal inducements offered to Catholics to change their religion were based, not on spiritual values, but on the ambition to own and to rise in the social scale. Consequently when the material condition of a younger son or brother improved by his conformity no one – least of all Protestants – concluded that he had taken that step to save his soul. 'I have lived here, where we are at least three-fourths Papists, going on twenty-seven years, in which time I have never heard of a convert upon principle. There are frequent legal converts . . .' declared Chief Baron Bowes in 1753.[5] Seeking to serve God and mammon set a problem which one woman solved by employing another to impersonate her and obtain a certificate of conformity. Others like Dr Fitzpatrick, the friend of Samuel Johnson, outwardly conformed and made a death-bed return. Johnson may have been thinking of Fitzpatrick when he referred to 'the laceration of mind' which conformity involved. The same mental conflict runs through the thought of Piaras Mac Gearailt:

> 'Tis sad for me to cleave to Calvin or perverse Luther, but the weeping of my children, the spoiling them of flocks and land brought streaming floods from my eyes and descent of tears . . . There is a part of the Saxon Lutheran religion which, though not from choice, I have accepted that I do not like—that never a petition is addressed to Mary, the mother of Christ, nor honour nor privilege nor prayers, and yet it is my opinion that it is Mary who is . . . tree of lights and crystal of Christianity, the glow and precious lantern of the sky, the sunny chamber in the house of glory, flood of graces and Cliona's wave of mercy.[6]

Some were like Joseph Blake whose case was submitted to Rome in 1765. He had gone to the warden of Galway and

5. Ball, *Judges*, II, 153-4.
6. Cf. Corkery, *The Hidden Ireland*, 283-5.

'testified from his soul' that he was a Catholic 'though afraid to confess it lest he should cause ample property coming to him in his hereditary right to be lost'. His petition for a dispensation for the marriage to his cousin which he had clandestinely entered was refused and he was warned against feigning another religion.[7] Others solved the difficulty like Luke Netterville, brother of Viscount Netterville of Louth. In 1725 he informed the House of Lords that he was the only Protestant in his family, having conformed in 1707 and educated his children in that religion. Consequently he was 'abandoned by all his Popish relations and thereby left to struggle under the extremest want and utmost necessity'.[8] It is not breach of charity to assume that the overwhelming majority were actuated simply by temporal motives, and differed chiefly from their Catholic neighbours in the greater looseness of their principles.

To win the Irish people to protestantism presented formidable difficulties. John Wesley put his finger on one of them when surveying the situation after half a century of anti-Catholic rule:

> At least ninety-nine in a hundred of the native Irish remain in the religion of their forefathers. The Protestants whether in Dublin or elsewhere are almost all transplanted from England. Nor is it any wonder that those who are born Papists generally live and die such, when the Protestants can find no better way to convert them than penal laws and acts of parliament.[9]

Even were the Protestant clergy to show zeal to evangelize it is highly questionable if a mass-movement of Papists would have been welcomed by the small ruling caste because of the redistribution of property and privilege that such a movement would involve. Consequently they preferred to

7. MacLysaght, 'Report on documents relating to the wardenship of Galway in *Anal. Hib.* 14, 87-8.
8. *Lords' Jn. Ire.*, II, 818.
9. *Journal*, III, 314.

tolerate an inferior class of citizens and to close their eyes to their religion provided there was no change in or danger to the *status quo*. But in order that they might live safely with the dangerous, untrustworthy political system they believed catholicism to be, the strict control, and ultimate elimination, of the Catholic hierarchy and clergy was a first objective.

THE EPISCOPAL SUCCESSION

The popular notion of the priest of the penal days as a hunted man, going about in disguise under an assumed name, rests on truth, but not the whole truth. Priests were fugitives, went in disguise, and used fictitious names, but not habitually. It would appear from Bolton's *Justice of the Peace for Ireland* that in the seventeenth century priests were normally charged under the Elizabethan Acts of Supremacy and Uniformity, which were adequate to cover an accusation of exercising priestly functions. In 1605 James I by proclamation expelled bishops and 'all Jesuits, seminary priests and other priests ordained by any authority from Rome'. Proclamations in 1673, 1674 and in 1678 appear to have been the first to distinguish between archbishops, vicars general, abbots, dignitaries, Jesuits and other regular priests on the one hand, who were ordered to depart the kingdom, and secular priests on the other, who were not named in the proclamation.[1] Similarly the first special legislation of the penal code against the clergy, contained in 9 Will. III, c.1, *An Act for banishing all Papists exercising any ecclesiastical jurisdiction, and all Regulars of the Popish clergy out of the Kingdom* before 1 May 1698, did not affect secular clergy who were not bishops, vicars general or dignitaries.

It seems to have been so generally accepted that the passing of this act would make it quite impossible for any person known to be a bishop either to remain in Ireland or to enter the country from abroad that a rather extravagant suggestion

1. Burke, *Penal times*, 39, 41, 52.

to outwit the law was put to the Pope. This was to send two bishops to Ireland through Germany, Holland or Portugal, states which had diplomatic relations with England. Under great secrecy they would interview bishops-elect on the continent or in Ireland; but they would consecrate them only in Ireland. Of the consecrators, one, a foreigner ostensibly travelling for health reasons, could claim his own nationality if intercepted. The other, however, would have to be Irish, to act as guide and interpreter. He could travel in the role of companion or servant, but would be in reality a bishop with the title of patriarch, so that, if arrested, he could claim that his office was not mentioned in the Act of Banishment. The proposal was not adopted, nor, as events were to show, was anything so elaborate ever needed.[2]

With the death of Archbishop Brenan of Cashel in 1693 the hierarchy in Ireland was reduced to Dr Phelan of Ossory who, like Dr Brenan, had ignored orders and temptations to quit the country during the Popish Plot scare. Dr Phelan died in January 1695. The consecration of John Sleyne for the see of Cork and Cloyne, which took place in Rome in September 1693, was timely. He was the consecrator of Edward Comerford for Cashel in 1697, and perhaps of Maurice Donnellan for Clonfert (1695), William Daton for Ossory (1696), Richard Piers for Waterford (1696), Patrick O'Donnelly for Dromore (1697), and Michael Rosseter for Ferns (1697).[3] Bishop Daton left Ireland in 1698, Bishop Piers in 1701; Dr Sleyne was imprisoned and the rest went underground. They were relentlessly pursued by the government, and when Dr Sleyne was finally sentenced to banishment in 1703 only three bishops were left in the country, Dr Comerford of Cashel, Dr Rosseter of Ferns and Dr O'Donnelly of Dromore.[4]

2. Ed. Giblin, 'Miscellaneous Papers', in *Archiv. Hib.* 16, 70-73 (1951).

3. Cf. Carte MSS 208 (Nairne Papers 1), nos. 19-27; Renehan, *Collections,* I, 464-5.

4. Burke, *Penal times,* 136-7; Moran, *Spicil. Ossor.,* II, 369-70. Very little is known of Bishop Rosseter, but he registered as parish priest of Killinick, co. Wexford, in 1704.

In 1707 James III, having now attained his majority, wrote
to Cardinal Imperiali, the protector of Ireland, of the
country's need of bishops. Of the two there, he said, one,
the bishop of Dromore, was in prison. The other, the archbishop of Cashel, was an invalid.[5] In 1707 Clement XI
nominated Edmund Byrne to Dublin, Hugh MacMahon to
Clogher, Ambrose MacDermott, O.P., to Elphin and
Thaddeus O'Rourke to Killala. Later in the same year
bishops were appointed to Meath, Achonry and Kilmacduagh. Dr MacMahon was consecrated at St Omer and Dr
MacDermott in Rome. The release of Dr O'Donnelly was
fortunate. On Sunday 24 August 1707 he was the consecrator
of Thaddeus O'Rourke for Killala, and on the following
Sunday of Edmund Byrne for Dublin. Bishops were
nominated to Ferns in 1709, to Cashel in 1711, to Cork and
Cloyne in 1712, to Tuam, Meath, Killaloe, Clonfert and
Ossory in 1713, and to Armagh and Kildare and Leighlin
in 1715.[6]

In almost every case, the documents of appointment of
these bishops record the candidate as 'nominated by the
king of England'. Nevertheless, the papacy did not recognize
the Old Pretender's right of nomination unambiguously until
1715,[7] and the cardinal protector maintained contacts with
the bishops and clergy in Ireland through the internuncio in
Brussels. Thus, for example, when the clergy of Ossory on
14 March 1712 petitioned for the appointment of their vicar
general, Patrick Shea, they pointed out that in addition to
his intellectual qualifications he had 'vigorously served in
this mission this fifteen years past, amid the several great
storms and persecutions that were contrived to suppress the
church, where he can continue in time of need, as being
qualified by his registry'.[8] A synod of Kilmore on 25
November 1715, petitioning for the appointment of Michael

---

5. *H.M.C. Cal. Stuart Papers,* I, 210.

6. See Ritzler-Sefrin, *Hierarchia Catholica,* V, under the respective dioceses.

7. For details concerning the papal grant of the right of nomination see ch·
III (Giblin, 'Irish exiles in Catholic Europe'), pp. 47-52.

8. Carrigan, *Ossory,* I, 143.

Smyth as bishop, stated that postulations had already been sent to Louvain in 1702, 1706 and 1712, but had not been sent to Rome. It was added that it was difficult and dangerous to have new priests ordained. The diocese was troubled by Calvinists and Jansenists, and torn by internal dissent, and a learned ruler acceptable to priests and people was needed.[9]

Bishops were nominated to Down and Connor in 1717, to Elphin in 1718, and to Derry, Kerry, Kilmacduagh and Limerick in 1720. Raphoe, which was without a bishop since 1661, was filled in 1725, and a vacancy in Kilmore since 1669 ended in 1728.[10] This brought the hierarchy almost to full strength. The futility of the Banishment and Registration Acts was shown by the appointment of so many bishops, two of them being Franciscans and four Dominicans. However, the identity and activities of bishops still needed elaborate protection. It was normal that Irish bishops be granted a dispensation allowing them to be consecrated by one bishop assisted by two priests, so that they might be consecrated with as little risk as possible. Elaborate care was also taken in the ordination of priests to conceal the identity of the ordaining bishop even from the priest being ordained, as an Act of 1709 (8 Anne, c. 3,25) makes clear:

> Whereas they have conferred the popish holy orders on popish priests who were not popish priests at the time of the registring, which they perform by laying on of the hands of many of the popish priests together to the intent that the party himself so receiving the said holy orders may not know in whom the power of conferring such popish holy orders was lodged . . .

These precautions were effective in assuring the episcopal succession during the first quarter of the century, when the penal code was at its most oppressive.

9. McKiernan, 'Father Michael Smith, a candidate for the diocese of Kilmore', in *Breifne* 1, no. 4, 387-93 (1961).

10. Ritzler-Sefrin, *op. cit.;* for the Kilmore appointment see also Fenning, 'Michael MacDonogh, O.P., bishop of Kilmore 1728-46', in *I.E.R.* (series 5) 106, 138-53 (Sept. 1966).

Jacobite nominations continued until the death of the Old Pretender in 1766, influencing indirectly the attitude to the *de facto* regime of Irish clergy who ambitioned promotion or had secured it already. By reason of their continental connections many Dominicans and Franciscans were consistent Jacobite supporters and the Pretender showed his appreciation by nominating considerable numbers from each order to Irish bishoprics. The attachment to the Stuarts of Thomas de Burgo, O.P., bishop of Ossory (1759-76), is well known. Instances of such loyalty from earlier in the century are perhaps less well known. For example, Ambrose O'Connor, the Dominican provincial, seems in 1708 to have been at least as interested in gathering political and military information for the Stuart cause as in visiting his province.[11] When Catholics were suffering particularly harsh treatment immediately after the accession of George II in 1727, Lord Delvin drew up an address of loyalty which he proposed the Catholics should sign and present to the king. At first a considerable number of signatures was obtained in Dublin, but the project was opposed by Francis Stuart, the Franciscan provincial, and even more sharply by another Franciscan priest, Sylvester Lloyd, both of whom later became bishops. Their opposition led many to withdraw their support from Delvin's project, and in the end his address was left with only a handful of signatories.[12] Until church-state relations have been thoroughly investigated it must suffice to say that, whatever the private sentiments of the majority of the Catholic clergy and laity may have been, they counselled, however grudgingly, obedience to the *de facto* regime which gave them no reason for regarding it with enthusiasm.[13]

11. Cf. Fenning, 'The Irish Dominican province under appointed superiors (1698-1721)', in *Archivum Fratrum Praedicatorum* 38, 310 ff (1968).

12. Brady, *Eighteenth-century press,* 45-6; Giblin, 'Catalogue Nunz. di Fiandra', in *Coll. Hib.* 5, 121-2 (1962); Stuart to James III, 9 March 1728, printed in O'Laverty, *Down and Connor,* V, 534.

13. Cf. the rather ambiguous statement in Dr O'Reilly's *Catechism* (c. 1726): '[The fourth commandment] obligeth us besides to pay honour and obedience to all our superiors, whether spiritual or temporal, in all things lawful, and not otherwise.'

With the gradual restoration of the hierarchy went a certain
reorganization of the dioceses. Cashel and Emly were united
in 1718. Ross was given in administration to Cork and Cloyne
in 1733, but in 1747 Cork became an independent diocese
and Cloyne and Ross were formally united. Three years later
Kilfenora was given in administration to the bishop of
Kilmacduagh, with the proviso that after his death the rule
of the joint dioceses should rotate between a bishop of
Kilfenora and a bishop of Kilmacduagh. In 1756 Ardagh
and Clonmacnois were formally united.[14]

THE CONDITIONS OF EXISTENCE

Important in the eyes of the law though the bishops were,
they were only a handful; but the clergy were a ubiquitous
problem. The enactment of the banishment legislation was
made easy for William by the treaty of Ryswick in 1697
which left him less dependent on the Emperor Leopold, his
Catholic ally. Two months before the day fixed for the
departure of the clergy Leopold instructed his representative
to notify William that by consenting to such legislation he
contradicted his promise to the emperor and violated the
treaty of Limerick. Even if William did not intend to enforce
it, there was no guarantee that his successors would not do
so. Diplomatic complaints were met with diplomatic
explanations; but nothing was done to suspend the
expulsion.[1]

Meanwhile hurried preparations were made for the fatal
day. A proclamation of 5 February 1698 stated that the
bishops had been busy ordaining priests, especially regulars,
to put them in parishes and thereby evade the law, and that
many bishops would change their names and addresses and

---

14. Ritzler-Sefrin, *op. cit.*, V, VI, under the respective dioceses.

1. Walsh, 'Glimpses of the penal times', in *I.E.R.* (series 4), 27, 606-18 (June
1910); Fenning, 'The Irish Dominican province under appointed superiors
(1698-1721)', in *Archivum Fratrum Praedicatorum* 38, 273 ff. (1968).

remain. The 1704 Registration[2] reveals the names of twenty-three priests ordained in 1697 and of seven in 1698, by the bishops of Clonfert, Cork, Ossory and Waterford. Three weeks before his departure the bishop of Ossory left books, vestments and religious ornaments in safe keeping in Kilkenny 'in case there be any prospect that the church should flourish'. Making preparations for the day of return, the Franciscans arranged to send novices abroad in the care of older members and to appeal to the government on behalf of aged and infirm friars. They left their possessions with benefactors, as did also the Augustinians and Dominicans.[3] Some 444 clergy are recorded as having been transported from the ports of Dublin, Galway, Cork and Waterford in 1698,[4] and there may have been departures from other ports. Appeals on their behalf by the Holy See were generously answered in Italy, Austria, France, Flanders, Spain and Portugal.[5]

The fact that there were no nuns in Dublin may perhaps be the reason why they are not mentioned in the anti-Catholic enactments under William and Anne. Even in pre-reformation Ireland nuns had been relatively few, not because women were less sensitive than men to the call of the religious life, but because they were hindered by social and economic barriers which narrowed the scope of their activities and their means of support. Communities of nuns were of course abolished in Ireland at the dissolution of the monasteries, but early in the seventeenth century girls from Ireland began to join religious institutions on the continent, where the developments in post-reformation days gave new scope for their activities within the cloister. A few groups returned to Ireland and managed to maintain themselves there with difficulty, but at the beginning of the eighteenth century they

2. Ed. Walsh, in *I.E.R.* 12 (1876).

3. Carrigan, *Ossory,* I, 128; Burke, *Penal times,* 129-31; Giblin, *Liber Lovaniensis,* xxi, 225-6; Fenning, *art. cit.,* 272 ff.

4. Burke, *Penal times,* 132; Renehan, *Collections,* I, 84.

5. Cf. Moran, *Spicil. Ossor.,* II, 347 ff.

were reduced to two small communities, Dominicans in Galway and Carmelites in Loughrea.

During the very first years of the penal code quite a number of young women appear to have entered the religious life on the continent,[6] and before long new convents were being set up in Ireland. The Poor Clares, who had re-established themselves in Galway, came to Dublin in 1712 at the invitation of Dr Nary, the parish priest of St Michan's. It was a bold move, and shortly after their arrival the nuns were arrested. There was no concealing the fact that they were nuns, but as no law could be cited against them they were discharged.[7] About five years later a group of Dominicans from Galway also came to Dublin, moving into the house in Channel Row which the Irish Benedictine Dames of Ypres had occupied for a brief period in the reign of James II.[8]

Incidents such as the thwarting of the attempt to found a convent at Clonmel in 1713 and the attack on the houses in Galway the following year showed, however, that their legal security might yet be threatened.[9] Legislation against nuns was proposed in 1719 and 1723. That of 1723 contained the clause 'to suppress all Popish nunneries . . . we pray that it may be further enacted . . . that from and after 25 March 1724 . . . no Papist keep any boarding-school or place for the reception of women . . . to be dieted and educated'.[10] The dropping of these bills assured the nuns of a reasonable security: for the future they were able to live the religious life without any notable subterfuge. There may be indications that it was considered prudent to refer to their establishments as 'boarding-schools' rather than as 'nunneries'; as the draft

6. For help given to them by Mary of Modena between 1695 and 1701 see *H.M.C. Cal. Stuart Papers,* I, 96, 100, 104, 109, 117-18, 124-7, 130, 132, 134, 140, 145, 152-4, 167.

7. Brady, *Eighteenth-century press,* 18; Moran, *Spicil. Ossor.,* III, 153; Meagher, 'Glimpses of eighteenth-century priests', in *Rep. Novum* 2, no. 1, 130 (1957-8).

8. Fenning, 'The Irish Dominican province under appointed superiors (1698-1721)', in *Archivum Fratrum Praedicatorum,* 38, 333-5 (1968).

9. Burke, *Penal times,* 352, 415.

10. *Ibid.,* 459.

legislation of 1723 makes clear, the nuns had even by this date undertaken the education of girls. In this, too, they continued unmolested.[11]

The Report to the House of Lords in 1731[12] provides a record of further foundations. It lists one nunnery in Drogheda, three in Galway, Dominicans, Franciscans and Augustinians, and one of Carmelites in Loughrea. Each of these four orders had a house in Dublin. There is 'a reputed nunnery' in Cork, two rather uncertain references to 'nunnerys' in the diocese of Clogher, and the testimony of the Protestant archbishop of Tuam that in his diocese 'several nuns live singly with relatives and friends'. While the penal code remained in force there were few additions to the convents of nuns mentioned in this list. The great expansion was to begin only at the end of the eighteenth century, with the native foundations which were to contribute so much to the development of the church not only in Ireland but in the whole English-speaking world.

That many priests defied the order to leave is clear from prosecutions during the next few years, from the proclamations against fugitives and their protectors, and from the declarations of the government that more stringent laws were necessary against those who remained or returned.[13] A report in March 1701 tells of 'the late return of thirty-six banished clergy into one county, and of the continuation of many popish bishops, vicars general etc., who shelter under the notion of popish priests'.[14] An address to parliament in 1703 tells how visitors and regulars conceal themselves

under the guise of physitians and other professions; and

---

11. Cf. Brady, *Eighteenth-century press,* 51, 60, 65, 85; Mac Fhinn, 'Scríbhinní i gCartlainn an Vatican', in *Anal. Hib.* 16, 173-80 (1946).

12. Published as 'Report on the state of Popery in Ireland, 1731', in *Archiv. Hib.,* I-IV. For references to convents of nuns see I, 11-12; II, 131; III, 126, 133, 153; IV, 132, 141. See also Kingston, 'The Carmelite nuns in Dublin (1644-1829)', in *Rep. Novum* 3, no. 2, 331-60 (1963-4).

13. See Walsh, 'Glimpses of the penal times', in *I.E.R.* (series 4) 22, 66-89, 244-68 (July, Sept. 1907), 25, 393-407, 503-12, 609-25 (April, May, June 1909).

14. 'Memorandum of Edward Lloyd', in *Cal. S.P. Dom., 1700-02,* 285.

others who by reason of their age and being better
known cannot conveniently conceal themselves rather
than leave the kingdom chuse to abide imprisonment,
where by interest of their gaolers, they easily obtain
leave to teach as school masters, and have their daily
Masses, and thereby all desired opportunity of ordaining
others; and otherwise propagating and perpetuating
their dangerous idolatry.[15]

It is clear from the 1704 registration list that the bishop of
Cork, who was in prison from 1698 till his transportation in
1703, ordained at least three in 1698, one in 1699, two in
1700 and five in 1701.

Conscious of its failure to control the increase of the
clergy the government decided to face up to the situation and
permit a limited number of seculars to remain under rigid
conditions. Such priests were obliged to attend the local
quarter sessions between 24 June and 20 July 1704, stating
their names, places of abode, ages, parishes, where, when and
by whom ordained (2 Anne c.7). They were also to provide
two sureties of £50 each to be of peaceable behaviour and
not to remove from the county of residence into another.[16]

Without delay the ecclesiastical authorities secured the
first advantage in an effort to outwit the law. Because most
Catholic parishes at this time were unions of smaller civil
parishes, they were able to secure a legal footing for a
considerable number by registering priests for areas that did
not represent the existing territorial arrangement. Thus in the
city of Dublin alone thirty-four priests were registered.
Elsewhere a few priests without parishes were registered, one
of them being 'infirm and weak'. Registration appears to
have been refused in some few cases, but in general the
authorities seem to have facilitated those who wished to
come within the law. In all, 1,089 registered, and some of

15. *The humble address of John Whaley to the Lords spiritual, temporal and
Commons, printed at the Crown in Patrick St.,* Dublin 1703.

16. Ed. Walsh, 'An Act for registering the Popish clergy', in *I.E.R.* 12, 299-312,
338-60, 376-408, 420-56, 464-500, 512-50 (1876).

them can be identified as Augustinians, Dominicans, Franciscans and Jesuits. There was one Cistercian. The only three bishops in the country, Drs Comerford, Rosseter and O'Donnelly, registered themselves as parish priests.

Of the 1,089 priests named in the registration list 252 were returned as having been ordained abroad, from which it may be taken as certain that they had studied outside Ireland (though of course one may not conclude that a priest ordained in Ireland had not studied abroad, for in the late seventeenth and eighteenth centuries it was a common practice that a young man be ordained priest in Ireland and then sent to the continent to complete his ecclesiastical studies). In the majority of cases, however, the priests returned as having been ordained abroad came from counties with shipping contacts with the continent, as Cork (27), Dublin (32), Galway (17), Kerry (27), Limerick (22), Waterford (14) and Wexford (23). Out of 189 registered for the nine counties of Ulster, only nine were ordained abroad.

The act was to remain in force for five years, during which age, infirmity and death would have made a big reduction because it was intended that there should be no succession. Further legislation in 1709 (8 Anne, c.3) closed several loopholes. Under heavy penalties, no parish priest might in future keep a curate, nor might he officiate outside the parish for which he was registered. Within the limits of his parish the registered priest might legally say Mass, confer the sacraments and minister to his flock; but there were certain functions that he might perform only at his peril. If he reconciled a Protestant to catholicism he incurred the penalty of *Praemunire* (2 Anne, c.6), and quite a number of priests were imprisoned for this offence.[17] The priest who officiated at the marriage of a Catholic and a Protestant, or of two Protestants, was even more bitterly pursued. After 1 November 1707 he was made liable to imprisonment and transportation, even if he was unaware of the religion of the parties he had married (6 Anne, c.16). Legislation in this

17. Cf. Brady, *Eighteenth-century press*, 47-50.

matter continued until 1750: in the end the law declared such a marriage void and the priest officiating liable to the death-penalty (19 Geo. II, c.13). There are indeed instances of priests being executed for performing marriages of this kind, even before the death-penalty was formally attached to the offence by law, for it aroused such feeling in Protestants that a priest so charged who failed to surrender for trial could find himself proclaimed as 'a tory, robber and rapparee in arms and on his keeping', and therefore faced with a capital charge when brought to trial and indeed liable to be killed out of hand without any trial at all.[18]

Even if he tried to minister quietly in the parish for which he was registered and kept a wary eye on every oppressive law, the priest could find disaster descending from quite unexpected quarters. Legislation designed to protect the property of Protestants laid down that, provided the property owner could swear that the damage he had suffered was the work of Catholics, compensation was to be levied from the Catholics of the locality. Writing in 1714, Bishop MacMahon of Clogher records a case where the registered Catholic priest was gaoled until his parishioners had paid the levy in full.[19] The gravest disadvantage a priest suffered from being registered was that he was now well known to the authorities should they wish to take any action against him.

New legislation introduced in 1709 obliged the clergy to take an oath before 25 March 1710, denying that the Pretender, who had recently come of age, had any right or title to the English throne, declaring that Anne was lawful and rightful queen, that the succession belonged to the Protestant line, and that such acknowledgement was made 'heartily, willingly and truly', under penalty of losing the limited right allowed by law to registered priests. Although the clergy were at the disadvantage of being known to the

18. *Ibid.,* 45, 57, 62; Burke, *Penal times,* 187 ff., 397; Walsh, 'Glimpses of the penal times', in *I.E.R.* (series 4) 30, 145-58 (Aug. 1911); Brady, 'Archbishop Troy's pastoral on clandestine marriages', in *Rep. Novum* 1, no. 2, 482 (1956).

19. Moran, *Spicil. Ossor.,* II, 472.

B

civil authorities, when the fatal day came less than thirty-five priests had taken the oath, which in the meantime had been condemned by Rome.[20]

Their refusal to swear arose from conscience rather than from political attachment. Anne had not endeared herself to them, but they remained aloof from the political intrigues to put her step-brother on the throne. They were prepared to recognize her as *de facto* ruler, but halted at declaring that a successful revolution had made what was now *de facto* also *de iure*. And to whom would they owe their allegiance if another successful revolution brought a Catholic successor to Anne? As the politicians knew, this was not a remote possibility. Nevertheless it was decided to go ahead and enforce the act.

Ten weeks after it had come into force it was reported that no Mass had been said in Dublin during that time because the archbishop and clergy had gone into hiding and because sixteen non-juring priests were then in Newgate gaol. The pattern of enforcement varied throughout the country, depending on local conditions ranging from active hostility to friendly sympathy.[21] The names of humane Protestants of this era are remembered with gratitude in Catholic tradition.[22] Conditions in Ulster were particularly difficult for priests and people. In 1714 Bishop MacMahon described them as follows:

> During these years a person was afraid to trust his neighbour lest, being compelled to swear, he might divulge the names of those present at Mass. Moreover, spies were continually moving around as Catholics . . . Greater danger threatened the priests as the government

20. Brady, *Eighteenth-century press,* 13; Giblin, 'Catalogue Nunz. di Fiandra', in *Coll. Hib.* 4, 118 ff. (1961); Burke, *Penal times,* 197, 245, 464 ff.; Wall, *The Penal Laws,* 20-21.

21. Burke, *Penal times,* 208 ff.; Walsh, 'Glimpses of the penal times', in *I.E.R.* (series 4) 26, 293 (Sept. 1909).

22. Burke, *Penal times,* 179, 194 ff., 243, 312, 370.

persecuted them unceasingly and bitterly, with the result that priests have celebrated Mass with their faces veiled lest they should be recognized by those present. At other times Mass was said in a closed room with only a server present, the window being left open so that those outside might hear the voice of the priest without knowing who it was, or at least seeing him. And herein the great goodness of God was made manifest, for the greater the severity of the persecution, the greater the fervour of the people. Over the countryside people might be seen, on meeting, signalling to each other on their fingers, the hour Mass was due to begin, so that people might be able to kneel and follow mentally the Mass which was being said at a distance. I, myself, have often said Mass at night with only the man of the house and his wife present. They were afraid to admit even their children, so fearful were they. The penalty for allowing Mass to be celebrated in one's house is £30 and imprisonment for a year.[23]

Safeguarding the identity of the priest and congregation had been made necessary by a section of the 1709 Act which empowered any two magistrates to summon any Catholic of sixteen and upwards and question him on oath as to when and where he was at Mass, by whom the Mass was said, and the names of the congregation. Refusal to attend or answer was punishable with imprisonment of twelve months or a fine not exceeding £20, payable to the parson and church-wardens for the poor of the parish, thereby tempting them to become informers.[24]

This period too saw the emergence of the professional 'priestcatcher', who made a living by collecting the rewards the law offered to 'discoverers' of priests. The two most prominent priestcatchers were Edward Tyrrell and John

23. Moran, *Spicil. Ossor.*, II, 473.
24. Brady, 'Magistrates' questions to Catholics, 1709', in *Archiv. Hib.* 24, 199–200 (1961).

Garzia.[25] Tyrrell, a renegade Catholic, was executed for bigamy in May 1713. Garzia, a Jew from Spain or Portugal, had a longer run. He arrived in Dublin in 1717 and began work immediately. However, his zeal led to a situation highly embarrassing to the government, for in June 1718 he made a capture which included Edmund Byrne, the archbishop of Dublin. The archbishop was finally put on trial only in November 1719, and as Garzia did not put in an appearance in court he was discharged. There can be no doubt of considerable foreign diplomatic intervention in the archbishop's interest, and the plain fact was that the government was not prepared to face the consequences of putting him on trial simply that a man like Garzia might collect his reward.

Over the next three or four years Garzia gradually disappeared from the Irish scene. His repeated petitions for money showed that the priestcatcher's trade had brought only limited rewards. He complained too, of the dangers he had to face from 'the fury and malice of the Papists'. He was not the first to find the calling a dangerous one. In 1711 the priestcatcher Henry Oxenard had nearly lost his life in Dublin under the 'stones, brick batts and dirt' thrown by the 'rioters or Popish mob'.[26] In 1707 the house and property of Richard Huddy of co. Cork was set on fire and destroyed because he had 'brought to justice one William Hennessy, a regular of the Popish clergy'.[27] The priestcatcher had to face contempt as well as danger. In law he was a 'discoverer', but it was the term 'priestcatcher' which stuck, and even among Protestants it soon became a term of contempt and common

25. Brady, *Eighteenth-century press*, 15, 21, 29, 34; Burke, *Penal times, passim;* Moran, *Spicil. Ossor.*, III 131-2; Giblin, 'Catalogue Nunz. di Fiandra', in *Coll. Hib.* 5, 83 (1962); McGrath, 'John Garzia, a noted priest-catcher, and his activities, 1717-23', in *I.E.R.* (series 5) 72, 494-514 (Dec. 1949); Donnelly, *Dublin parishes*, pt. 6, 40-46; Wall, *The Penal Laws*, 31-3; Walsh, 'Glimpses of the penal times', in *I.E.R.* (series 4) 29, 128-45 (Feb. 1911), 30, 369-87, 509-25, 570-76 (Oct., Nov., Dec., 1911).

26. Brady, *Eighteenth-century press*, 15-16.

27. *Ibid.*, 9; Burke, *Penal Times*, 213; Walsh, 'Glimpses of the penal times', in *I.E.R.* (series 4) 30, 161-2 (Aug. 1911).

abuse.[28] No decent man, whatever his religion, could approve
of the priestcatcher, and certainly no decent man became one.

The framers of the Registration and Abjuration Acts were
reluctant to admit defeat and they were slow to realize that
uniform enforcement needed an efficient body to operate the
laws, together with the sympathy of the people. Both factors
were seldom present. The legislative and executive bodies
were independent of each other and did not necessarily work
in unison. Two-thirds of the population was Catholic and a
large number of the remainder were Presbyterians, also
harassed by the laws because of their beliefs. When in 1712 a
constable executing the warrant to arrest the ninety-year-old
dean of Armagh summoned aid from the civilian population,
it was reported that they, 'amongst whom were some
Dissenters', absolutely refused to assist him.[29] It is difficult
to say how long the active campaign to impose the oath
lasted, but Lord Chancellor Phipps, addressing the lord
mayor and corporation of Dublin in January 1714, complained of their laxity in terms which suggest that any
concerted attempt at enforcement had been dropped: 'The
country generally make the city their pattern, and after your
example become negligent of their duty in this aspect; for
being asked why they permit public Mass to be said the
answer is, " 'tis done in Dublin . . ." '.[30] Faced with apathy
from its own class and with opposition from the majority of
the people, the government, recognizing its helplessness,
quickly ceased to insist on the oath except as a safety measure
against fears of Jacobite uprisings.

Sporadic enforcement continued, depending very much on
the temper of the local magistracy.[31] Times of political unrest,
such as 1715, saw renewed outbursts against Popery, and it
took time for the ferocity of the persecuting spirit to die.
Anti-popery legislation drafted in 1719 and 1723 contained

28. Brady, *Eighteenth-century press*, 89; Burke, *Penal Times*, 236-7.
29. Brady, *Eighteenth-century press*, 19.
30. *Ibid.*, 22.
31. *Ibid.*, 15, 24-6; Burke, *Penal times, passim*.

such barbarous proposals as that of whipping nuns in 1719 and in the Bill of 1723 against unregistered priests, which, in Lecky's phrase, 'deserves to rank with the most infamous edict in the whole history of persecution'. In both years diplomatic intervention in London by the Catholic powers, made at the request of the Holy See, helped to avert the threat of new legislation.[32]

Without the steadfast support of the laity the clergy could not have survived these bitter years. It is clear from the 1704 registration list that many priests lived with their relatives or friends outside the parishes for which they registered. The list also shows men like John Brown of Neale, co. Mayo, acting as surety for seven priests, and Thady Rody of Crossfield, co. Leitrim, the patron of native learning, surety for four. They were not isolated cases. Unlike the laity, the priest had little of the world to lose beyond his liberty, but the laity sheltered, protected and rescued their clergy regardless of the cost to themselves.

Just as it is not the whole truth to see the priest of the penal days simply as a man hunted by the law, neither is it the whole truth to see the Catholic laity as an undifferentiated mass of 'poor people used worse than negroes by their lords and masters, and their deputies of deputies of deputies'. Nevertheless, the Catholic laity too lived within an elaborate framework of law, designed, if not for their destruction, at least for their effective exclusion from any kind of social status, from education, from professions, and above all from the ownership of land. In 1703 Catholics still held 14 per cent of the land; three-quarters of a century later they held only 5 per cent.[33] The reduction had been brought about by the operation of laws designed to make it almost impossible to hold on to property except at the price of conformity to the Protestant church. Another set of laws prevented Catholics from taking property except on short and disadvantageous

32. Brady, *Eighteenth-century press*, 40-41; Giblin, 'Catalogue Nunz. di Fiandra', in *Coll. Hib.* 5, 89 ff., 109 ff., 156 ff. (1962).
33. This is the estimate of Arthur Young, *A Tour in Ireland*, II, pt. 2, 44.

leases. If a Catholic secretly purchased property, the first Protestant to inform against him became proprietor. This was even more lucrative than priestcatching, and naturally bred a race of 'discoverers' who jealously watched for any attempt at evasion. Legislation in 1778 allowed Catholics to take a lease of 999 years or five lives, and four years later, in 1782, further legislation in effect put an end to any discrimination.[34]

The penal code left one means of amassing wealth open to Catholics, not so much because it was overlooked as because it was despised. No law effectively prevented the rise of Catholic merchants and traders. By the closing years of the seventeenth century Catholics had become prominent in Irish trade, and even in the first quarter of the eighteenth, Protestants were not disposed to challenge them there. A Protestant made money from trade in order to buy land, which of course was not possible for Catholics. Almost by legal compulsion, the Catholic merchant lived quietly and unostentatiously, with the result that about 1770 a strong urban middle class had developed, deriving on the one hand from the dispossessed gentry, who did not scorn to hold on to wealth by means of trade, and on the other from industrious apprentices, of whom John Keogh was perhaps the most famous, who were proud of being the founders of their fortunes.[35]

The political rebirth with which these merchants were so particularly associated was very remote from the first quarter of the century, when almost the only weapon left in Catholic hands was the fury of the mob. This, however, could be an effective weapon. It had been a deterrent to the professional priestcatcher, and the magistrate too zealous in enforcing the anti-popery laws could feel it as well. It might be that the mob's efforts were frustrated, as happened in the attempt to rescue Dean McGurk in 1712 (the old man died early the

34. Meagher, 'Of the genus called "Discoverer" ', in *Rep. Novum* 1, no. 2, 443-60 (1956).
35. Wall, 'The rise of a Catholic middle class in eighteenth-century Ireland', in *I.H.S.* 11, 91-115 (Sept. 1958).

following year in Armagh gaol),[36] but they could also be
successful, as witness the rescue of the friar James Kilkenny
in Roscommon in 1715. In this case, some of his rescuers
were prosecuted, and one, a woman, fined £20,[37] but it was
not easy to get convictions and the arrest of priests could
always be a hazardous business.

What is perhaps the most interesting testimony to the
constancy of the Irish Catholics in the grim days of the early
eighteenth century comes from a rather unexpected source.
A number of Catholic missionaries returning from China in
an English ship were weatherbound for months off the west
coast of Ireland and spent some time in the port of Galway.
One of them, John Mezzafalce, gave a long account of what
he had seen in a letter to the Pope which may be dated 1708.[38]
He spoke of the

> constancy and devotedness with which they adhere to
> the Holy See, proclaiming their faith in the presence of
> heretical officers and ministers . . . And this protestation
> of faith was not confined to words, but was also set
> forth in their actions . . . though they were ridiculed and
> laughed at, yet they all faithfully observed the fast and
> abstinence . . . In order to hear Mass on Sundays and
> holydays, the men and women go out from the city, for
> Mass is not permitted within the city walls . . . however
> within the city itself several persons have secretly their
> chapels where Mass is privately said . . . This constancy
> amid so many persecutions is quite general and shared
> by almost all of every condition and sex and age . . . As
> they learned that there was a bishop, Mgr Maigrot, on
> board, they came in crowds, in small boats, men and
> women, from the city and the adjoining country, all
> asking for the bishop's blessing. The heretics being

36. Burke, *Penal times,* 282-3.
37. *Ibid.,* 451; Brady, *Eighteenth-century press,* 24; Walsh, 'Glimpses of the
penal times', in *I.E.R.* (series 4) 30, 159 (Aug. 1911).
38. Moran, *Spicil. Ossor.,* II, 395-8.

enraged at this, in order to strike them with the greater
terror a colonel of the army who happened to be on
board, struck violently a noble and well-educated youth
named Gregory French who asked 'ubi est Dominus
episcopus?' . . . All this however did not deter the good
Irish people from again coming on board, and even when
Mgr Maigrot exhorted them to beware of exposing
themselves to the like insults, they at once replied
'Romani sumus et nihil timemus. . . .'

It is hard to improve on Lecky's verdict:[39]

Under the long discipline of the penal laws the Irish
Catholics learnt the lesson which, beyond all others,
rulers should dread to teach. They became consummate
adepts in the arts of conspiracy and of disguise. Secrets
known to hundreds were preserved inviolable from
authority. False intelligence baffled and distracted the
pursuer, and the dread of some fierce nocturnal venge-
ance was often sufficient to quell the cupidity of the
prosecutor. Bishops came to Ireland in spite of the
atrocious penalties to which they were subject, and
ordained new priests. What was to be done with them?
. . . The administration of the law was feeble in all its
departments, and it was naturally peculiarly so when it
was in opposition to the feelings of the great majority
of the people. It was difficult to obtain evidence or even
juries . . . as it was quite evident that the bulk of the
Irish Catholics would not become Protestants, they
could not, in the mere interests of order, be left wholly
without religious ministration.

In this context, a point may be made here, though its full
treatment belongs to the chapter on Catholic Relief. As
early as 1723 members of the legislature showed themselves

39. Lecky, *Ire.,* I, 167-8.

conscious of the political dangers arising from the continued allegiance of the Irish Catholics to a Church proscribed by law.[40] A series of proposals between this date and the late 1750s outlined a plan to allow permanently 'a competent number' of secular priests and even a few bishops, provided they accepted a measure of government control. None of these proposals proved acceptable to the government. When emancipation came, it took the form prefigured in the Oath of Allegiance of 1774, namely political emancipation and religious toleration involving no obligation on the part of the Catholic Church towards the state. A few minor vexatious restrictions remained for the secular clergy – for example, they might not assume ecclesiastical rank or title, nor appear in ecclesiastical dress outside their places of worship, which were not to have bell or steeple. The restrictions on the regular clergy were more serious: in effect, their legal proscription remained. But the laws against them had long been inoperative; indeed after 1750 their strength in Ireland was threatened by legislation from Rome rather than from Dublin.

PASTORAL REORGANIZATION

At very much the same time as the government was declining any part in the organization of the Catholic Church in Ireland, the Church itself was trying to put its affairs in order. At the centre of this reorganization was a set of Roman decrees drawn up in 1750 and published early in 1751. To understand the problems they dealt with, it will be necessary to examine the grave difficulties facing the pastoral mission in Ireland in the first half of the eighteenth century.

Following the Banishment Act of 1698 there was a great exodus of regular clergy, and the bishops in Ireland were reduced first to four, and later, for a while, to two. Replace-

40. See Brady, 'Proposals to register Irish priests', in *I.E.R.* (series 5) 97, 209-22 (April 1962).

ment of vacancies among the parochial clergy was difficult,
and in order to make provision for the community at large
those in authority in each diocese appear to have availed of
the terms of the Registration Act to arrange that regulars be
registered in fictitious Catholic parishes.[1] During the next
twenty years active enforcement of the laws against unregistered priests gradually lessened, regulars returned in
growing numbers, and the hierarchy was substantially
restored. Although their legal status remained so long
unchanged, the clergy were in practice more and more
unmolested. Even during the great scare of 1745, when the
order was given to put the popery laws fully into execution,
it was complied with in a desultory way which suggested that
the priests were not really considered to be a political threat.

The gradual restoration of the hierarchy made possible a
progressive reorganization of church life and revival of
church discipline, both of which had been disrupted since
the close of the seventeenth century. The bishops in exile
presumably made provision for administration during their
absence, but the canonical status of priests who ruled sees
that were long vacant was often uncertain. It would appear,
for example, that for a time the vicar general of Clonfert
also ruled Elphin, and an appeal has survived from one of
his decisions to the vicar general of Tuam as representative
of the absent metropolitan.[2] Uncertainty was all the greater
when a number of rivals claimed to govern, as happened in a
number of dioceses about this time, especially in the northern
province. During the seventeenth century it had been claimed
that the archbishop of Armagh as metropolitan and primate
had the right of providing for the interim rule of vacant
suffragan sees, and when Armagh itself was vacant its care-
taker claimed that the same rights extended to him. Given
the difficulty of maintaining bishops in the northern province
at the beginning of the century, it is not surprising that there
were many disputes between rival authorities, notably in

1. See above, p. 16.
2. Burke, *Penal times*, 250.

Armagh, Kilmore and Derry.[3] But as more and more dioceses came to have a resident bishop, no longer could there be any doubt as to who was in authority, or what was the source of his jurisdiction.

Within his diocese, the bishop had to organize a system of pastoral care. It was not easy. The list of 1,089 'registered parish priests' in 1704 does not, of course, mean that at that date there were 1,089 stable parishes in the country. The Ferns diocesan statutes of 1722 show that the parochial system was in many ways very unstable. Some of the parish priests at any rate had no fixed residence. In some cases the vestments, chalices and other things needed for public worship were in the hands of the laity, who had taken them for safe-keeping when times were even worse, but who were unwilling to restore them to the clergy now that some kind of parochial system seemed to be taking shape. One revealing statute orders a priest who has accepted a parish to serve in it for at least a year, and if he decides to vacate it he is obliged to give the bishop six months' notice of his intention.[4] There is no reason to believe that conditions in Ferns were any worse than those in the south of the country generally, but it is clear that the parochial system existing there in 1722 was still far from stability.

Nevertheless, a system was gradually established. This brought new problems. The means of livelihood of most of the clergy being uncertain and meagre, the canonical right to a parish was important and so was often a matter of contention. Regulations made for Dublin in 1730 ordered that a parish could only be acquired by collation and renewal of faculties. Similar provisions appear for Cork in 1768.[5]

3. See Bishop MacMahon of Clogher to Propaganda, 1714, in Moran, *Spicil. Ossor.*, II, 481 ff., and further correspondence in Giblin, 'Catalogue Nunz. di Fiandra', in *Coll. Hib.* 4, 108-9, 125 (1961). For some of the problems in Kilmore see Fenning, 'Michael MacDonogh, O.P., Bishop of Kilmore 1728-46', in *I.E.R.* (series 5) 106, 141 (Sept. 1966).

4. Corish, 'Ferns diocesan statutes, 1722', in *Archiv. Hib.* 27, 76-84 (1964).

5. Moran, *Spicil. Ossor.*, III, 141-2; *Statuta synodalia pro dioecesi Corcagiensi*, Cork 1768.

Episcopal collation was sometimes resisted, especially when a bishop who was a religious could be accused of favouring one of his order by granting him one of the richer parishes in the diocese.[6] Clerics also turned up claiming a parish on the strength of a bull of provision from the Datary in Rome, which was sometimes issued on a very superficial examination of the facts of the case in distant Ireland.[7] Sometimes the situation was further complicated by the emergence of a kind of 'lay patron', either a Catholic who had built the Mass-house or the local Protestant magnate who was sometimes prepared to tolerate a secular priest but not a religious. It was not unknown for a section of the congregation to seize the Mass-house for a priest of its own choice. Among the clergy, *esprit de corps* was sometimes lacking and grievances were brought before the civil or even the Protestant ecclesiastical authorities.[8]

In the nature of things, the bishop found great problems in exercising his authority. His legal position obliged him to avoid the notice of magistrates and to rely on the loyalty and goodwill of his flock rather than on his authority over it. At the beginning of the century it was not uncommon for the bishop to live under an assumed name, but no matter what safeguards he took he was doomed to live precariously. On a number of occasions bishops were denounced to the magistrates by priests whom they had disciplined and although such denunciations became more and more an embarrassment to the administration it was a long time before the element of danger disappeared completely. In 1734 the archbishop of Cashel reported that there was a state

6. For an example of a very serious dispute in Kilkenny between the clergy and the Dominican bishop see Fenning, 'John Kent's report on the Irish mission, 1742', in *Archiv. Hib.* 28, 94 (1966); Giblin, 'Catalogue Nunz. di Fiandra', in *Coll. Hib.* 10, 77 ff. (1967).

7. For a problem under this head in Mullingar in 1739 see Giblin, 'Catalogue Nunz. di Fiandra', in *Coll. Hib.* 10, 82 ff. (1967), and for problems in Dublin in 1744 see *ibid.*, 99.

8. For some examples, see Burke, *Penal times,* 172, 217-19, 289; *Archiv. Hib.* 3, 125; Renehan, *Collections,* I, 105; MacFhinn, 'Scríbhinní i gCartlainn an Vatican', in *Anal. Hib.* 16, 188 ff. (1946).

of terror because a priest in Cork, dismissed because of his scandalous life, had gone to the civil authorities and denounced his bishop as a Jacobite agent, and alleged that a papal bull had been sent to the Irish bishops granting a plenary indulgence to all who should contribute to the Jacobite cause. As a result, many chapels had been closed and the clergy had gone into hiding. In the same year the hue and cry was raised for Bishop Gallagher of Raphoe and some of his clergy because he had tried to expel a priest who had intruded himself into a parish. This priest had appealed to the magistrates, and the bishop's parish priest was taken. The people had rescued him from his captors, but in the struggle he had been mortally wounded.[9] As late as 1751 Bishop Sweetman of Ferns was brought to Dublin and interrogated at length in consequence of political charges brought against him by a refractory priest.[10]

The bishops also had to struggle with poverty. The Congregation of Propaganda seems to have accepted only with reluctance the practice whereby the bishop retained a parish as part of his episcopal *mensa*,[11] though it was pointed out that as well as providing the bishop with his only secure sustenance this retention of a parish also afforded legal concealment of his episcopal status. In some dioceses, it was difficult for a bishop to reside permanently. On a number of occasions in the first half of the eighteenth century Propaganda considered it necessary to speak harshly of Irish bishops who did not reside in their dioceses.[12] Some, the Congregation complained, lived on the continent on the fruits of some benefice they had obtained there.[13] There is, however, no evidence that this abuse existed on any serious

9. Giblin, 'Catalogue Nunz. di Fiandra', in *Coll. Hib. 9*, 40 ff. (1966).

10. Burke, *Penal times*, 315 ff. See also Wall, *The Penal Laws*, 40.

11. For the case of Archbishop Linegar of Dublin in 1734 see Giblin, 'Catalogue Nunz. di Fiandra', in *Coll. Hib.* 9, 39 (1966).

12. Cf. Mac Fhinn, *op. cit.*, *Anal. Hib.* 16, 167-8, 181-3; Renehan, *Collections*, I, 468-9; Moran, *Spicil. Ossor.*, III, 164-78; Wall, *The Penal Laws*, 41-2.

13. Giblin, 'Catalogue Nunz. di Fiandra', in *Coll. Hib.* 9, 49-50 (1966).

scale. Only a few bishops are named, and of these only one seems to have been without any excuse for his absence, the others being either too old and ill to return to the hardships of the Irish mission, or too badly compromised by their known allegiance to the Jacobite cause.

Of the bishops living in Ireland, there were some who as a rule resided outside their dioceses, apart from a formal visitation during the summer months. These also were not as numerous as the complaints of Propaganda might suggest, and there was usually a reason for their non-residence. In dioceses without a sizeable town, or in those with a particularly active magistracy, it might at times be difficult to find a place of residence where a bishop might live with the legal anonymity which was so desirable.[14] For reasons such as these we find bishops who seem to have made their permanent residence in Dublin, where it was so much easier to pass unnoticed. Bishop O'Shaughnessy of Ossory (1736-48), a native of Connacht and a Dominican, spent most of his life in the west of Ireland, either with his relatives or in Dominican houses.[15] While accepting the validity of the reasons given for non-residence of this kind, one can also understand the anxiety of the Roman authorities to end the practice. Partly because of Roman pressure, and partly because of improving conditions in Ireland, it ceased to be a problem after 1750.[16]

During the latter half of the seventeenth century provincial synods enacted for the country as a whole a considerable corpus of laws which remained in force or were renewed during the following century. In spite of their precarious

14. For an example, see Fenning, 'Michael MacDonogh, O.P., Bishop of Kilmore 1728-46', in *I.E.R.* (series 5) 106, 142 (Sept. 1966).

15. Carrigan, *Ossory,* I, 155; Fenning, 'John Kent's report on the Irish mission, 1742', in *Archiv. Hib.* 28, 94 (1966), and 'Some problems of the Irish mission, 1733-1774', in *Coll. Hib.* 8, 70 ff. (1965).

16. As late as 1768 the secretary of Propaganda complained to Archbishop Fitzsimons of Dublin that it was alleged that Irish bishops did not reside in their dioceses except when collecting offerings from parish priests (Curran, 'Archbishop Carpenter's *Epistolae,* (1770-1780)', in *Rep. Novum* 1, no. 1, 155 (1955). It is hard to see evidence to sustain such a charge at this date.

existence, the bishops of the early eighteenth century did succeed in holding a number of diocesan synods. What appears to be the earliest legislation from a member of the eighteenth-century hierarchy was issued in 1712 'with the consent and approval' of the clergy of Dublin.[17] In six brief rules it set out the rights and duties of parish priests and provided for the saying of Mass and the administration of the sacraments by clergy who had been approved by two of the parish priests. One of these, of course, was Archbishop Byrne, who had been registered in 1704 as parish priest of Francis St., but for security reasons his name or office was not mentioned. (Indeed, the occasion for drawing up this document may have been the need for the archbishop to go into hiding in the year 1712.) Before long, however, we find more formal diocesan legislative enactments, for example in Limerick (1721), Ferns (1722), Dublin (1730), Cashel (1737), Kildare and Ossory (1748).[18] The bishops were slower to hold provincial synods. One was held in the province of Tuam in 1752, and there were three in this province before 1770, but in the other provinces it does not seem to have been considered prudent to hold provincial synods, at least formally designated as such, until Catholic relief was well in prospect.[19]

Meetings of the clergy in the form of conferences were well organized from an early date. Sometimes they were held four times a year, but the more normal practice was that the clergy of each deanery met monthly during the six months of good weather. The purpose of these conferences was to keep the clergy in touch with their professional studies by the discussion of questions in dogmatic and moral theology and in canon law. Diocesan statutes laid down that all

17. Moran, *Spicil. Ossor.,* III, 128-9.

18. Begley, *Limerick,* 184; Corish, 'Ferns diocesan statues, 1722', in *Archiv. Hib.* 27, 76-84 (1964); Moran, *Spicil. Ossor.,* III, 139-47; Renehan, *Collections,* I, 465-7; Comerford, *Kildare and Leighlin,* I, 79-82; Carrigan, *Ossory,* I, 152.

19. Cf. *Archiv. Hib.* 5, 149, 153; Curran, 'Archbishop Carpenter's *Epistolae* (1770-1780)', in *Rep. Novum* 1, no. 2, 395 (1956).

priests exercising the care of souls should attend, though there are occasional complaints like that of the archbishop of Tuam in 1770 that 'the regular clergy are ordered to present themselves and they sometimes do'.[20]

Perhaps the gravest charge brought against some of the bishops in the beginning of the eighteenth century was that they ordained indiscriminately all who presented themselves without enquiring too closely into the needs of the mission or the candidate's qualifications or dimissorials. Their motive, it was alleged, was only too often the fee levied for this exercise of pontifical functions. Again, it must be emphasized that the bishops named as guilty of this irregularity (and in most cases the charges against those named seem to be proved) were a small minority of the episcopate. On the other hand, their irregular ordinations certainly seem to have been on a scale sufficient to create a serious pastoral problem. That a Jansenist agent could arrange for the ordination by an Irish bishop of twelve candidates on dimissorials from the chapter of Utrecht during 1714 and 1715 shows how necessary it was for the nuncio in Brussels to remind the Irish bishops two years later to exercise caution in their choice of subjects for ordination.[21] The Report of 1731 noted that, during the reign of Anne,

> the titular bishops ordained all persons, that could pretend to read Latin, without any other qualification; so that the popish priests grew scandalous by their number, ignorance and immorality . . . . But it is now a matter of favour to obtain orders even with a strict injunction to travel immediately . . . some bishops are suspended for ordaining and several priests excommunicated for not travelling . . .[22]

20. Cf. *Archiv. Hib.* 5, 133, 146, 150, 154; Moran, *Spicil. Ossor.,* III, 142; Curran, *art. cit.,* 395.

21. Clark, *Strangers and Sojourners at Port Royal,* 211-14; Moran, *Spicil. Ossor.,* III, 131-2.

22. 'To travel', i.e., to a continental seminary to study theology. The extract is quoted from *Archiv. Hib.* 2, 117.

C

The tone was hostile, and the condemnation of the harried bishops of Anne's reign too sweeping, but the assertion that the practice had ceased by 1731 was not altogether true. In 1734 accusations were made against the bishop of Achonry for alleged irregularities in ordaining candidates, and there seems no doubt of his guilt.[23] Earlier, the bishop of Killaloe had been reported to Rome by the internuncio in Brussels in 1723 for carelessness in this matter. He was suspended and the archbishop of Cashel appointed administrator of the diocese.[24] In 1729 the archbishop of Armagh complained that Bishop Flynn of Ardagh ordained all who presented themselves provided they paid him.[25] The legacy he left to his successor may be gauged from a respectful obituary notice of the latter in a Dublin newspaper of 1739:[26]

What is most observable in this illustrious defunct's character is, that during the eight years of his being bishop he never ordained one, and often bemoaned some of his confreres, who are too ready to impose hands on all sorts of unworthy subjects, and multiply the ministry to its dishonour, at a juncture when the whole kingdom is overstocked with clergy, and swarms of fryars who overburden the poor of their persuasion.

Other bishops were of the same mind. It was at the instance of the bishops of Kerry and Cork that the Holy See by a rescript of 7 April 1742 limited the faculties of each Irish bishop to ordain no more than twelve candidates *titulo missionis* during his episcopate.[27] Some restriction may have been necessary in the circumstances, but this particular decision was far too rigid and inflexible. It took no account of the fact that the *titulus missionis* was the only title of

23. Giblin, 'Catalogue Nunz. di Fiandra', in *Coll. Hib.* 9, 35 ff., 46 (1966).
24. A.V., Sec. Brevium 2606, ff. 9, 11.
25. Giblin, 'Catalogue Nunz. di Fiandra', in *Coll. Hib.* 9, 14 (1966).
26. Brady, *Eighteenth-century press,* 60.
27. Cf. Moran, *Spicil. Ossor.,* III, 161-2 and Mac Fhinn, 'Scríbhinní i gCartlainn an Vatican', in *Anal. Hib.* 16, 166 (1946).

ordination in Ireland, or of the considerable variations in
the size and needs of the different dioceses, but until the
Propaganda records have been fully studied it is impossible
to assess its effects exactly, or to establish with certainty the
extent to which it was in fact insisted on.

The regular clergy too survived their much more rigorous
proscription. As has been seen, though many were deported
under the Banishment Act of 1698, some remained to register
as parish priests under the Act of 1704. It is quite clear too
that non-registered religious remained – we know, for
example, that there were about ninety Dominicans in Ireland
in 1703, and it seems certain that only a minority of these
registered in the following year.[28] Though the penalty for
returning to Ireland was death, this was not in fact enforced,
and many religious did return. The Franciscans had to hold
their chapter in Louvain in 1700, but thereafter they met
regularly in Dublin, except in 1714, when the situation was
particularly bad, but even in that year the provincial superiors
nominated by the Pope were able to meet in Dublin to
choose the guardians.[29] The Dominicans, who in the beginning of the eighteenth century had had their provincials
nominated by the master general, regained all their rights as
a province in 1721. By this date it would appear that they
had succeeded in sending friars to Ireland in sufficient
numbers to maintain the strength they had in 1703.[30] In 1733
the Irish Capuchins became for the first time an independent
province.[31]

In some respect, the religious superiors faced even greater
problems than the bishops, for neither their subjects nor
themselves had any legal standing. At the beginning of the
century, community life in any real sense was out of the
question, and the nine Dominican communities mentioned

28. Fenning, 'The Irish Dominican Province under appointed superiors
(1698-1721)', in *Archivum Fratum Praedicatorum* 38, 290 (1968).

29. Giblin, *Liber Lovaniensis*, 243 ff.

30. Fenning, *art. cit.*, 342 ff.

31. Fenning, 'Some problems of the Irish mission, 1733-1774', in *Coll. Hib.*
8, 75 (1965).

in Connacht in 1703 must have been very rudimentary indeed.[32] By about 1720, however, community life became possible again, even in Dublin. That the law connived at its development is clear, for example, from the Galway sheriffs' tongue-in-cheek report in 1731 that they had searched the 'reputed friary' of the Augustinians in Galway, 'but could not find or discover any of the said friars', which contrasts pleasantly with the entry from the Augustinians' house-book indicating that they had treated the sheriffs to a bottle of wine on the occasion (the Dominicans, not to be outdone, had provided two bottles, 'to treat the sheriffs in their search').[33]

A measure of prudent concealment was still necessary, of course, and at times 'the restoration of the community' meant that a group would set themselves up on a farm in a reasonably remote place, and in this way manage to follow a community life.[34] Novices were concealed under the guise of hired 'servant-boys'. Before long complaints are to be heard that some of these farmers employ an excessive number of servant-boys. The complaints come almost simultaneously from the foreign friaries, who object to having so many of these young men sent on to them to complete their novitiate,[35] and from the Irish bishops, whose complaint is that too many receive final profession and holy orders without any proper novitiate.[36] There can be no doubt of the widespread practice of receiving novices rather indiscriminately. The Irish provincials of the religious orders denounce it severely, but like every ecclesiastical superior at the time they had to move with caution and do not seem to have been able to impose an effective curb on local superiors. Grave difficulties arose from the practice of nominating a titular superior to every religious house which had existed in pre-reformation times.

32. Fenning, 'The Irish Dominican Province under appointed superiors (1698-1721)', in *Archivum Fratrum Praedicatorum* 38, 290 (1968).

33. Wall, *The Penal Laws,* 53.

34. Burke, *Penal times,* 312 ff.

35. *Ibid.,* 258-9.

36. *Ibid.,* 259.

In consequence, many with the juridical status of guardian were in fact wandering friars who tried to bolster their shadow-jurisdiction by accepting novices as personal dependents. The situation was worsened by the fact, already noted, that some Irish bishops were prepared to ordain indiscriminately any candidate presented to them.

The Report of 1731 lists fifty-one friaries. There is reason to think the number somewhat exaggerated, but the number of friars listed, 254, is almost certainly an underestimate, if only because it was impossible to enumerate the friars unattached to any genuine community. What is clear is that the increase in the number of the friars and the fact that many of them were not under the effective control of the provincial superior posed grave difficulties for the bishops who were now trying to restore a working parochial system.

In effect if not in intention the different legal treatment meted out to secular and regular clergy had the result of sharpening their antipathies. These were further exacerbated by the fact that in early eighteenth-century Ireland both regular and secular depended on the offerings of the people. This led to a not always edifying competition to provide pastoral services, in which the confusions of the situation further complicated the legal problem of reconciling the tridentine concept of the office and powers of a bishop, limited though these had been by 150 years of further legislation, much of it tending to strengthen the central authority of Rome, with the wide faculties often granted to the regulars as 'apostolic missionaries'. These tensions appeared very clearly in the conflict which developed from the rather unreal claims advanced by the Canons Regular in the early eighteenth century.[37]

The Canons Regular of St Augustine had been very

---

37. For some of the documentation on the Canons Regular see Mac Fhinn, 'Scríbhinní i gCartlainn an Vatican, in *Anal. Hib.* 16, 166 ff. (1946); Moran, *Spicil. Ossor.,* III, 148-9, 176; Meagher, 'Glimpses of eighteenth-century priests', in *Rep. Novum* 2, no. 1, 144-5 (1957-8); Fenning, 'John Kent's Report on the Irish Mission, 1742', in *Archiv. Hib.* 28, 97-8 (1966); Giblin, 'Catalogue Nunz. di Fiandra', in *Coll. Hib.* 9, 60, 65 (1966), 10, 94-5 (1967).

powerful in pre-reformation Ireland, and had impropriated
a great number of parishes. Religious life among them
appears to have been at a low ebb, however, and when
pressure came they put up very little resistance to the
reformation. In 1646, as part of the hopes raised by the
Confederation of Kilkenny, a 'Congregation of Canons
Regular of St Patrick' was established. It was affiliated to
the Canons Regular of the Lateran in 1698. After the
Restoration of 1660, the Irish canons had established
themselves at Cong in the diocese of Tuam, and exercised
what seems to have been a contentious claim to four parishes
of the diocese. In 1703 Miles Burke, with the title of abbot of
St Thomas, Dublin, was appointed vicar general of the
congregation for Ireland, England and Scotland. Henry
Kelly was appointed his successor in 1729, and began to
advance claims based on the pre-reformation possessions of
the canons. When he came to Ireland in 1736 he tried to put
these claims into effect in Dublin, and raised fears that they
would be extended to the whole country. These fears very
quickly prompted a joint petition from the archbishops of
Dublin, Cashel and Tuam, the bishops of Ferns, Kildare,
Ossory, Meath, Kilmore, Ardagh and Elphin, and the
provincials of the Franciscans, Carmelites, Augustinians and
Dominicans, to have silence imposed on the claimants.

Though Henry Kelly failed to establish himself in Dublin,
the canons had powerful protectors in Rome. On 4 June 1741
their authority over the great pilgrimage-centre of St Patrick's
Purgatory was confirmed. Here too they failed to establish
themselves, and their claim became in effect confined to
Tuam. A further Roman decision of 12 March 1742 seems to
be at the same time a diplomatic recognition that the canons
had over-reached themselves and an attempt to make
provision for the existing members. Their postion in Dublin,
Tuam and Clogher was supported (in Dublin and Clogher
they had in fact failed to make it good), but a decision on any
wider claims was suspended and they were forbidden to
receive novices. As they were only sixteen in number, and had
had to send prospective recruits to the Irish college in Paris

for theological education, this decision was in fact a death-sentence. In 1755 they reached agreement with the archbishop of Tuam. No doubt the dispute would not have dragged on so long had it not been for their protectors in Rome, but the reaction in Ireland would scarcely have been so strong were it not for the confusions of the pastoral mission in Ireland, and in particular the bishops' sensitivity to any threat to the struggling parochial system.

The Roman decrees of 1750-51 may be said to have settled the issues between the bishops and the friars. The series of events leading up to them may be traced back to a letter written from Dublin in 1738 by someone who signed himself 'Paulus Benignus'.[38] He wrote, he said, on behalf of the *zelanti* of Dublin, to ask Propaganda to remedy a situation in which the Charter schools[39] were sapping the faith of the poor, who were being neglected by a disorganized clergy under bishops who too frequently were non-resident.

Propaganda reacted by seeking information from the nuncio in Brussels. He in turn wrote to a trusted correspondent in Ireland. This correspondent is not named, but was almost certainly a priest or a bishop. He had a gloomy story to tell. The Charter schools, he said, were a very serious threat indeed, which must be met by setting up Catholic schools; but the religious instruction of the people could not be organized while so many bishops were absentees — he names six in all whom he accuses of this fault.

Little action could be taken during the year 1740, six months of which were devoted to the election-conclave of Pope Benedict XIV. Information piled up, however, with the nuncio in Brussels and with Propaganda in Rome. The new Pope showed a keen interest in Irish problems. A distinguished canonist, he was determined that there should be a thorough reform. It was decided to send a visitator to Ireland, and John Kent, president of the Irish college in

---

38. For a summary of these events see Fenning, 'John Kent's Report on the Irish Mission, 1742', in *Archiv. Hib.* 28, 59 ff. (1966).

39. The Charter schools are treated below, pp. 73-5.

Louvain, was there in that capacity from July to September
1742. He spent most of this time in Dublin and Waterford,
so that much of his report to Propaganda must have been
based on hearsay evidence. It is a fairly severe indictment,
especially of the regular clergy, but while it is admittedly to
some extent biased there is no reason to believe it was untrue
in any matter of substance.

At any rate, it formed the basis for a set of decrees drawn
up by Propaganda in 1743. These were particularly restrictive
of the regular clergy, and no doubt it was because of the
weight of their objections that they were not put into effect.
Propaganda's second attempt to deal with the problem was
delayed because of the '45 and the disturbed years which
followed. The second set of decrees, finally issued in 1751,
withdrew some of the restrictions on religious proposed in
1743, but added another which was even more far-reaching.

Before studying the remedies, however, we are now in a
position to assess the state of the pastoral mission as disclosed
by all these enquiries. As Propaganda had already as interim
measures warned the bishops of their duty of residence (1739)
and restricted their right to ordain (1742), the main outstanding question was the deployment of the existing force
of clergy. Were there enough parishes? Were there too many
priests, and in particular were there too many religious
priests?

The statistics available are neither complete nor fully
coherent. To begin with, 1,089 'parish priests' registered in
1704. Of these, some were in fact regulars, while an indeter-
minate, though possibly sizeable, number of regulars had
remained even though not registered. The 1731 Report
estimated that there were about 1,700 priests in the country,
of whom 254 were regulars (as already noted, this is certainly
an underestimate). In 1742 John Kent reported that there
were 600 parishes in Ireland; 700 secular priests, of whom 550
were parish priests; and almost 700 regulars, of whom fifty
had parishes. One can do little more than record an impres-
sion, but it would seem that all these figures are underestimates. On the other hand, the figures given in a report,

unsigned and undated, but obviously a comment by a regular on the 1751 decrees,[40] are almost equally certainly over-estimates—1,200 seculars, almost 1,000 regulars, and 1,500 parishes (the last figure is certainly exaggerated). From these rather unsatisfactory statistics, it might be concluded, however, with a reasonable degree of certainty that: (i) many parishes were too big, and there was need for either division or the appointment of additional curates; (ii) if properly distributed, the number of secular clergy was not greatly excessive; and (iii) the regulars had increased in number much faster than the seculars, and, given the fact that direct ministration among the people was almost the only work for a priest to do, if there were to be an organized parish system work was not available for the number of regular clergy in Ireland.

The tenor of the Roman decisions will perhaps appear most clearly if they are set out under three heads: (i) decrees made in 1743 and repeated in 1751; (ii) decrees made in 1743 but withdrawn, i.e., not included in the decrees finally published in 1751; and (iii) decrees added in 1751 to those made in 1743.[41]

The decrees in the first category were almost all concerned to limit the pastoral rights of the regular clergy, apart from an exhortation to the bishops to divide the bigger parishes or appoint additional curates (the slowness in adopting this seemingly obvious remedy for Irish problems arose from the fact that a 'registered parish priest' was forbidden by law to have a curate) and the note that secular as well as regular clergy returning to Ireland needed testimonial letters from the nuncio in the country where they had studied. Houses of the regular clergy in Ireland were to be given recognition only where the community life was lived according to rule. 'Undocumented' religious returning to Ireland were to be judged to have forsaken their order, and the bishops were to

---

40. Ed. Giblin, in *Archiv. Hib.* 16, 76-81 (1951).

41. For the 1743 decrees see Fenning, 'John Kent's Report on the Irish Mission, 1742', in *Archiv. Hib.* 28, 99-102 (1966), and for those of 1751 de Burgo, *Hibernia Dominicana,* 179-81 or Renehan, *Collections,* I, 468-70.

do their best to have them expelled from the country. 'Documentation', that is, letters of approval from the local nuncio as well as the religious superior, was to be produced to the bishop whenever a religious received an appointment in his diocese, and the bishop was to be told the exact place to which the religious had been assigned by this superior. The bishop, for reasons which he considered sufficient, might transfer a religious to another place in his diocese, but the religious superior might not transfer him without the consent of the bishop. It is clear that these regulations gave the bishops a control wider than that laid down in the general canon law even over religious living in what were recognized to be exempt communities.

The lot of the regular clergy as a whole was not greatly alleviated by the fact that certain decrees proposed in 1743 were, on maturer reflection, not issued in 1751. A proposal to exclude altogether from Ireland the Capuchins and the Calced and Discalced Carmelites was dropped, as was the attempt to put the nuns under the control of the bishops instead of the religious provincials. On the other hand, a new regulation added in 1751 proved very restrictive. It forbade religious superiors to receive novices in Ireland. In future, the habit could be given only in their foreign colleges, where, Propaganda said, their novitiate could be properly organized, and they were forbidden to return to Ireland until their studies were completed.

None of the other regulations added in 1751 was as far-reaching. All priests returning to the Irish mission had to have testimonials, not from the local nuncio, but from the nuncio in Brussels, 'qui missionibus Hiberniae praeest'. Each bishop was to report to him every two years.[42] On episcopal non-residence, what in 1743 had been a personal warning to four named bishops became a law obliging the metropolitan to

---

42. That this may not have been very effective may be suggested by the fact that there are now only twenty-two *Relationes Status* for Irish dioceses in the archives of Propaganda for the second half of the eighteenth century – see Fenning, 'A guide to eighteenth-century reports on Irish dioceses in the archives of Propaganda Fide', in *Coll. Hib.* 11, 19-35 (1968).

see that his suffragans reside in their dioceses. A further series of regulations did little more than remind the bishops of the general law in such matters as the approval of confessors or the censorship of books.

Though there were complaints from the Irish bishops over the next few years that regular clergy were slow in putting these decrees into practice, they do seem to have been very substantially observed, and to have led to a notable drop in the numbers of the religious. In 1767 the friars petitioned jointly for a relaxation. Their number, they said, had fallen to 231 Franciscans, 147 Dominicans, 68 Augustinians and 34 Carmelites. It was also complained that the bishops were culling the best from the religious houses to help to man the parishes, as they were entitled to do under the decree of 1751. Propaganda met their grievances to the extent of allowing the friars to receive novices in Ireland, but it refused any substantial modification of the rules governing their missionary activities.[43] In 1780 Archbishop Carpenter of Dublin was still insisting that there could be no effective control as long as the practice continued of nominating titular superiors to long-vanished houses. These superiors, he said, received novices who when professed might find that they would not be accepted by any existing community, and too often ended up as couple-beggars and apostates.[44]

It has already been suggested that the number of secular priests in the country about 1740 was not greatly in excess of the needs of the parochial ministry. It might be noted too that the decree of 1742, limiting the numbers that the Irish bishops were allowed to ordain, was not incorporated into Propaganda's final rulings in 1751, though it was not abrogated and continued in force. As early as 1748 it was asserted that it was already being widely ignored by the bishops, but the source for this statement is distinctly anti-

43. Fenning, 'Some problems of the Irish mission, 1733-1774', in *Coll. Hib.* 8, 85 ff. (1965); Walsh, 'Glimpses of the penal times', in *I.E.R.* (series 4) 30, 586-7 (Dec. 1911).

44. See his *Relatio Status* for that year, ed. Curran in *Rep. Novum* 1, no. 2, 395-6 (1956).

Roman, and must be treated with caution.[45] In 1751 the vicar general of Dublin, Dr Fitzsimons, said that for twelve years there had been no ordination in the diocese, and that regulars had to be put in charge of some parishes because of the shortage of secular priests, though in the very same year we find Dr Sweetman of Ferns visiting Dublin 'to ordain eleven or twelve young men' for the aged Archbishop Linegar.[46] A few years later Archbishop Butler's Visitation Book[47] shows him ordaining six priests at Thurles for the united dioceses of Cashel and Emly on 19 August 1759. These instances would seem to indicate that already in the 1750s the decree of 1742 was no longer being rigorously adhered to, and that either it was sometimes ignored or dispensations were fairly freely given, but the complaints of a general shortage of priests continue into the 1760s.[48] The available evidence is too scattered to permit of a firm conclusion, but it may be taken as certain that the decree did make it difficult to provide sufficient numbers for the growing needs of the parishes.

There is only scattered evidence also for any attempt to estimate the standard of education expected from Irish students in the continental seminaries, or of the amount acquired by them there. The provision of an efficient clergy from this source was one of the major aims of the counter-reformation in Ireland, but it was hampered by legal and financial difficulties. As in so many other matters, standards improved after 1750. For the sixteen years between 1751 and 1767 the regulars could recruit only through their continental colleges, and although the problem of the uneducated religious reappeared when they were again allowed to receive novices in Ireland it must have been on a comparatively

---

45. Cf. Fenning, 'Some problems of the Irish mission, 1733-1774', in *Coll. Hib.* 8, 79 (1965).

46. Burke, *Penal times*, 308, 316.

47. Published by Lenihan in the *Limerick Reporter and Tipperary Vindicator* between 7 Feb. and 1 Aug. 1873.

48. Cf. *Archiv. Hib.* 4, 39 (1915); Fenning, 'Some problems of the Irish mission, 1733-1774', in *Coll. Hib.* 8, 82, 85 (1965).

small scale. There was always a coming and going of clerics between Ireland and Catholic Europe. Such traffic was of course forbidden by law and not without risks, especially in the first half of the century. The commonest subterfuge seems to have been to describe the young clerics in terms which suggested that they were going abroad as apprentices to a trade. This was perfectly legal, and the presence of Irish merchants in many of the seminary towns of the continent lent further similitude to the deception. In 1725 we find a young Augustinian novice recommended to a foreign superior: 'he has a great inclination to become an apprentice in your house'.[49] Bishop Richardson of Kilmore, who died in 1753, left in his will 'sixty pounds to be employed in putting six young persons apprentices to such business as they may live by . . . four of the county of Cavan and two of the county of Leitrim'.[50] But notwithstanding such subterfuges the risk remained, and especially in time of international tension there was always the danger of being challenged at the ports. In the years after the '45 the letters of Thomas Hennessy, the Jesuit superior in Ireland, to the rector of Salamanca, are sprinkled with references to 'the landlord' [the bishop], 'our farm', 'our trade', 'our sinking trade' [the Jesuit mission in Ireland], and 'our factory' [the seminary in Salamanca].[51]

Many of these young men were already ordained priests before they went abroad. The practice was not welcome to the superiors of the seminaries, who would have preferred boys of sixteen or seventeen to be sent to them, as 'such young candidates have more time to prepare . . . their good and bad qualities are more thoroughly known; they have less opposition to the yoke of discipline and subordination; they are less exposed to the dangers of a precipitated choice

49. Burke, *Penal times,* 255.

50. Carrigan, 'Catholic episcopal wills: Armagh', in *Archiv. Hib.* 1, 184 (1912).

51. Corish, 'Correspondence of the superiors of the Jesuit mission in Ireland with John O'Brien, S.J., rector of Salamanca', in *Archiv. Hib.* 27, 85-103 (1964).

of a state in life'. There were also sound reasons, however, for sending young men of more mature years and even already ordained. Being ordained, they were able to make some contribution to their support during the period of their studies by the exercise of their priesthood. Of at least equal importance was the consideration that boys who left Ireland for a continental seminary at the age of sixteen or seventeen might return quite unfitted for the hardships of a priest's life in Ireland, if indeed they returned at all, whereas those leaving at a more mature age would have been already initiated into the Irish pastoral life by having been employed as catechists and teachers.[52]

It is possible to follow the workings of the system in some considerable detail in the diocese of Cashel, where it had been very thoroughly organized by the Butler archbishops. Archbishop Christopher Butler (1711-57) kept a strict watch and control over candidates for orders. From quite early in his episcopate he seems to have assembled them in a special school under his personal supervision.[53] His successor, the first Archbishop James Butler (1757-74), was also most meticulous in watching over candidates for orders. His practice, as his Visitation Books show, was to assemble them four times a year in Thurles for examination and instruction.[54] The investigation was very detailed, as will appear from the example of John Comin, who was examined by the archbishop in 1758. The report on this young man reads as follows:

> John Comin recommended by Rev. Tim MacCarthy for good morals and ingenuity; born 14 November 1734; . . . his first school master was Edmd. English of Duniskeagh with whom he spent 2½ years learning to read and write, and the most part of his grammar

52. Cf. Moran, *Spicil. Ossor.*, III, 162; Mac Fhinn, 'Scríbhinní i gCartlainn an Vatican', in *Anal. Hib.* 16, 164 (1946); Boyle, *The Irish College in Paris*, 35 ff.

53. Renehan, *Collections*, I, 304-5.

54. See also Renehan, *op. cit.*, I, 314-15.

afterwards; he spent 9 months with Malachy Dwyer learning Latin and spent 18 months with Patrick Patswell at Carrignashure. After that he spent 9 months with Tim Ryan at Sollihedbeg, and thence he went to the school of Edmd. Commen and spent two years with him learning Latin; he afterwards taught a public school for 7 years in the parish of Crook, the parish priest of which place, Rev. Thomas Hogan, by his certificate, 28 June 1758, sets forth the spiritual life and good morals of s^d Commine who declares its not Latin he taught for seven years but figures. S^d Commine spent 7 months with Jas. Cantillon at Dromculliher . . . during which time . . . [he] applys himself to Latin . . .

John Kavenagh from near Gorey, co. Wexford, kept a detailed and informative diary.[55] A farmer's son, he was born in 1749 and began his schooling at the age of five. It continued under a series of itinerant teachers of varying ability. One of them, 'a very profound Latin scholar and Grecist', was a clerical student until he lost an arm. During 1760 Kavenagh was so impressed by a requiem that he decided to become a priest. Between 1770 and 1774 he studied Latin under different teachers. In July 1774 his parish priest told him of Dr Sweetman's decision to ordain him. Meanwhile the priest taught him the breviary, and between 23 and 28 October he received minor orders, subdiaconate and diaconate. After ordination on 30 October 1774 he returned home to be instructed in the ceremonies of the Mass by his parish priest. This done, he was permitted by the bishop to say Mass for a month and he said his first in his father's house. This brief preparation for the priesthood clearly implied a further course in a seminary abroad. Three months seems to have been the period usually allotted to the young priest to betake himself to his further studies.[56] Kavenagh went to Nantes, and though he returned to Ireland in 1781 his brief stay

55. Now in the Library of the Passionist Fathers, Mount Argus, Dublin.

56. Cf. Renehan, *op. cit.,* I, 307-8.

shows that those whowent to the continent at a more mature age could be as disinclined to settle down at home as those who went as boys. In 1782 he was back in France as a chaplain to the French navy. He later returned to Ireland, and died as parish priest of Rathdrum, co. Wicklow.

Availing of the Relief Act of 1782 Catholics began to erect schools with elaborate programmes. An academy opened in Cork by a priest in February 1783 had Greek, Latin, Italian, French and Spanish on its curriculum.[57] Three years later another priest opened an academy for boarders at Tipperary in which Latin, Greek, French and Philosophy were taught.[58] A meeting of the bishops of Tuam province in 1786 decided to establish a seminary at Athlone for clerical students.[59] In Dublin Archbishop Carpenter opened a college in November 1783 under Frs Betagh and Mulhall. Dr Plunkett regarded it with such approval that he adopted it as a seminary for Meath and sent his clerical students there.[60] But by far the most important foundations were those at Kilkenny and Carlow, which later developed into the present colleges for ecclesiastics.

The legal permission to allow Catholics to open schools, even of limited resources and scope, was of considerable benefit to them and it prepared the way for the foundation of Maynooth College. This was the most significant event in Irish ecclesiastical history since the reformation and the decision to allow it was largely dictated by expedience. The outbreak of the French Revolution was a challenge to the established order, and the early fears of Irish priests coming from the continent as Jacobites now changed to a fear of them as Jacobins. The Irish bishops shared the government's anxiety on this point. They were not willing, they stated in 1794, to send youth abroad and expose them 'to the contagion of sedition and infidelity, nor their country to the danger of

57. Brady, *Eighteenth-century press,* 221-2.
58. *Ibid.,* 247-8.
59. *Ibid.,* 247, 264-5, 281.
60. Cogan, *Meath,* III, 138.

thus introducing the pernicious maxims of a licentious philosophy'.[61] This common interest of bishops and government made possible the foundation of Maynooth.

LIFE OF THE CLERGY

Little is known of the day-to-day lives of the clergy during the first quarter of the century and most of their activities are described in hostile sources. They were a *gens lucifuga,* avoiding attention, and some of their public statements counselling docility indicate how deeply their wretched conditions had depressed them.

Adversity shared in common with their people who sheltered and supported them with loyalty and generosity forged a deep bond of unity and understanding. For their part, the clergy were not unmindful of this and on the whole they did not betray the confidence of their flocks. But when a priest changed his religion the contempt of the layfolk was unmistakable. He was rejected by his relatives; he was ostracized by the people and lampooned in some of the bitterest poems in the Irish language.[1] The disappointment of his lapse was all the more galling because an early Act of Anne (2 Anne c.7,3) provided him with £20 a year to be levied off the people amongst whom he had lived. Even the legislators despised him; and although they later doubled that sum they placed more humiliating obligations on the recipient (8 Anne, c.3). At the end of our period, the apostasy of John Butler, bishop of Cork, and the circumstances attending it, caused widespread indignation. 'The populace were so shocked at it, that they gathered round his carriage and pelted him with all that came to their hands, so that had

---

61. Healy, *Maynooth College,* 657.

1. Of the many examples which might be cited, see Brady, *Eighteenth-century press,* 168-9, 197, 208; Wall, *The Penal Laws,* 39-40. Clerical apostasies also occasioned some very lively pamphleteering. Very little of the satirical poetry in Irish has been published. For an account of some such poems in B.M. Eg. MSS see *B.M. cat. Ir. MSS,* II, 54-5.

it not been for Lord Earlsford taking him into his carriage,
I doubt what would have become of him', wrote a con-
temporary.[2]

Protestant bishops regarded apostate priests with suspicion
and were slow to admit them amongst their clergy. Walter
Blake Kirwan was almost the only one to make a name for
himself in the Church of his adoption. The rest faded into
obscurity, some as teachers, others as couple-beggars, who
made a living by assisting at clandestine marriages. These
marriages were valid in civil law, though heavy penalties
were imposed on the priest who officiated at the marriage
of Protestants. The bishops were not in a position to impose
the tridentine law forbidding clandestine marriages among
Catholics for fear of complications with the civil law, and the
ecclesiastical penalty of excommunication invoked against
the couple-beggar and often against the parties he married
proved ineffective.[3] A living was to be had at the calling of
couple-beggar, though not a very honourable or decent one.
Such men led a degraded and often drunken existence, and
frequently fell foul of the civil law not only for assisting at
Protestant marriages but for other crimes as well. They
could often prove irrepressible. James Doyle was excom-
municated in 1751 by Bishop Sweetman of Ferns after a
stormy career which culminated in his denouncing his
bishop to the government as a Jacobite agent; twenty years
later the bishop was still issuing public warnings against him
as 'an infamous and incorrigible couple-beggar'.[4] 'Coghlan
the priest, the notorious couple-beggar' was indicted in
Dublin in 1753 for assisting at mixed marriages and sentenced
to be transported to the American plantations.[5] Of the same

2. Cf. Kingston, 'Lord Dunboyne', in *Rep. Novum* 3, no. 1, 62-82 (1962).

3. See Archbishop Carpenter's *Relatio Status* (1780), in *Rep. Novum* 1,
no. 2, 397-8 (1956); Brady, 'Archbishop Troy's pastoral on clandestine
marriages', *ibid.,* 481-5; Renehan, *Collections,* I, 437 ff.

4. Burke, *Penal times,* 315 ff.; Grattan-Flood, 'The diocesan manuscripts of
Ferns under the rule of Bishop Sweetman (1745-1786)', in *Archiv. Hib.* 3,
118-19 (1914).

5. Brady, *Eighteenth-century press,* 81.

stamp was Matthew O'Brien, 'a popish priest distinguished by the name of Father Tack'em', who was jailed in Kilkenny in 1771, charged with 'divers crimes'.[6] The most indestructible of them all, however, was Patrick Fay, a priest of the diocese of Meath. He conformed to the established Church in 1772 and married in 1776. In 1786 he was indicted for assault and sentenced to six months' imprisonment, which he talked his way out of. In 1788 he was sentenced to death for forgery. The sentence was commuted to transportation for life, and in 1789 he left for Botany Bay. Within a few years he had made his way back, for he had another brush with the law in Dublin in 1795. He ended his days quietly in co. Kildare.[7]

In the early decades the clergy lacked fixed residences and lived with relatives or friends. During the bitterest days of persecution under Anne, Fr Michael Plunkett of Meath lived with a friendly Protestant magistrate.[8] In 1711 the bishop of Ferns mentioned his intention of having houses built which would also serve as places where Mass could be said most furtively, but eleven years later, in 1722, it is clear that many of the priests of Ferns were still without a fixed residence.[9] Of an Ossory parish priest the Protestant bishop noted in 1732: 'I saw near his cabin some wheat that he was putting into a stack and several stacks of hay, from whence 'tis plain that he uses a farm.'[10] In Kerry at the middle of the century the earl of Kenmare encouraged clergy to build on his estates: 'It is right to set small lots to these parish priests as they are well able to improve them and their having houses of their own prevents their coshering and being an encumbrance on the houses of their parishioners.'[11] Parochial houses appear to have been normal throughout Cashel in 1754 and

6. *Ibid.*, 141.

7. For Fay see *Commons' jn. Ire.*, X, 270; Brady, *Eighteenth-century press*, 150, 232, 247, 260, 262-3, 266, 268, 294, 296.

8. Cogan, *Meath*, I, 269.

9. A.P.F., S.R.C.G. 610, f. 631; Corish, 'Ferns diocesan statutes, 1722', in *Archiv. Hib.* 27, 76-84 (1964).

10. Carrigan, *Ossory*, I, 148.

11. MacLysaght, *The Kenmare Manuscripts*, 222. Cf. also *ibid.*, 64, 202.

Archbishop Butler notes that after his visitation of two parishes some Protestants were invited to dine with the archbishop and clergy. Similar conditions obtained in Ferns where Dr Sweetman noted in 1753: 'I am always to dine at the pastor's house as frugally as he pleases. I am to recommend them a little decency in their habitation and dress',[12] though in 1744 a number of priests in Ferns are reported as still living with relatives or parishioners.[13]

A proposal in 1749 to oblige priests to wear distinctive and approved attire so that they might easily be recognized indicates that clergy and laity wore similar clothes.[14] This is confirmed by the apology of a footpad on discovering the identity of a priest whom he had just robbed.[15] Referring to the recommendation of the Council of Trent that clergy should wear distinctive dress, Archbishop Christopher Butler of Cashel stated:

> this order cannot literally be observed, but the spirit of it may, be keeping as close to it as times will permit, that is by contenting ourselves with the cheapest and most ordinary apparel; by this means a great deal may be spared for adorning our altars and chapels. What is more shocking and irreligious than to see a pastor of souls appearing abroad in cloth and linen of the finest, well mounted and accoutred and, a little after, perhaps, covered with a dirty and tattered alb and vestment, approaching to an altar decked with foul rags, a pewter chalice . . . ?[16]

12. Grattan-Flood, 'The diocesan manuscripts of Ferns during the rule of Bishop Sweetman (1745-1786)', in *Archiv. Hib.* 2, 101 (1913).

13. Burke, *Penal times,* 313-14.

14. *The Ax laid to the root, or reasons humbly offered for putting the Popish clergy in Ireland under some better regulations.* Cf. also Burke, *Penal times,* 461-3.

15. Brady, *Eighteenth-century press,* 230-31.

16. From the archbishop's pastoral letter known as the 'psalter of Cashel', summarized in Renehan, *Collections,* I, 305-10.

The clergy then wore the same dress as the laity, the priests in the country tending to wear the frieze of the peasantry, while the town clergy and the bishops tended to adopt the dress of the eighteenth-century middle-classes, from wig to buckled shoes. It was only at the very end of the century that priests began to dress in black. The Roman collar came even later, superseding the cravat. In 1792 Dr Plunkett of Meath gave a detailed description of a bishop's out-of-doors attire:

> I am in rags . . . I want a complete suit to appear in. The coat is to be fine cloth of that kind of blue that is tinged with purple. The last I had was rather coarse, and did not yield good service. The waistcoat fine Lutherine; and two pair of the best sattinett breeches . . . make the buttonholes strong, especially at the breast of the coat; and give me good buttons, those at the knees of the small clothes require to be of the most durable quality of silk or thread . . . I had two pair of bandages, of each pair one is now broken . . .[17]

Dr Plunkett had need of durable clothes. For many years, until his clergy presented him with a coach, he travelled the length and breadth of his extensive diocese yearly on horseback. This was the normal mode of travel and in 1764 it was an established custom in various dioceses that the horse, bridle and saddle of deceased parish priests should fall to the bishop. Archbishop Butler of Cashel who died in 1791 refers in his will to his post chaise and Dr McKenna of Cloyne who died in the same year mentions an 'old carriage'.[18]

In the stern days at the beginning of the century the worldly sustenance of priest or bishop could be very slender indeed. 'The priests tell me they are in very low circumstances. Some have not eaten meat for four or five months on end'

17. Cogan, *Meath,* III, 171-2.

18. Renehan, *Collections,* I, 106; Carrigan, 'Catholic episcopal wills; Cashel', in *Archiv. Hib.* 3, 163, 178 (1914).

wrote the bishop of Clogher in 1714.[19] However, an improvement came when the lives of the clergy settled into a pattern under the grudging toleration of the government. While there are references to payments in kind and references too to priests and even bishops[20] farming for themselves, the income of the priest was based on the offerings of his parishioners in the form of Christmas and Easter dues and fees paid on the occasion of his exercise of his priestly functions. The bishops lived from offerings of this nature from the parish or parishes they reserved for themselves and from the *cathedraticum,* an annual Easter payment from the clergy. Propaganda several times reproached the Irish bishops for retaining too many parishes for themselves. It is not easy to say what substance may have been in these complaints, but objections raised on the same occasions against the practice of the priests' receiving money when they conferred the sacraments showed a failure to appreciate that such 'stole-fees' could not be dispensed with under Irish conditions.[21]

Only very scattered references to the actual sums paid have survived. In Dublin city, where the clergy lived on their church-door collections, what is described as 'a poor parish' was reckoned in 1751 to be worth £50 or £60 a year to the parish priest after the curates' share had been deducted.[22] Archbishop Carpenter in 1780 said that few rural parish priests in his diocese could afford to keep a curate.[23] Under interrogation in 1751 Bishop Sweetman of Ferns said:

> In his parish some give him £5 5s., some £1 1s., some 6½d. In some parishes his priests only get corn and other little things. Collections of Sundays is for the priest. In his parish he gets half the collection and the priests the other half. He has thirty-two parishes. They give him a

19. Moran, *Spicil. Ossor.,* II, 471.

20. Cf. Carrigan, 'Catholic episcopal wills: Armagh', in *Archiv. Hib.* 1, 176, 179 (1912).

21. See above, p. 30, with the references given in note 12.

22. Burke, *Penal times,* 308.

23. *Rep. Novum* 1, no. 2, 394 (1956).

guinea each at the distribution of oyles, has not above
£40 a year from the parish, of which he gives one third
to the coadjutor. The collection at his chapel door is
about £16 a year. This is the best parish in his diocese
yet not above £40 a year, and some accidental things
about £10 a year. Common parishes worth about £30
or £35 a year and when he was a priest one year £30,
a second year £34, third year £42. And they all have
dependents.[24]

In 1785 his *cathedraticum* amounted to £62. 4. 11., in
1786 to £75. 19. 4.[25]

The author of *The Good Confessor,* writing in 1743, says
that the clergy should take only the fees fixed by the bishop,
or, failing this, fixed by diocesan custom. He mentions a fee
of a shilling for granting a certificate of marriage, and of
half-a-crown or three shillings for marriage-dues. He
complains, however, that some clergy exact a great deal
more.[26] Complaints of such clerical exactions came to the
fore in the Whiteboy agitation, and the controversies they
gave rise to provide some detailed accounts of the dues of
the clergy.

The Whiteboy movement began as an agitation against
the payment of tithes to the established Church. From the
beginning it was denounced as an unlawful conspiracy by the
Catholic authorities, all the more sharply as the Whiteboys
began to take advantage of the people's being gathered for
Mass as an occasion to force them to take the Whiteboy
oath. As hostilities between them grew sharper, the Whiteboys' demands came to include a protest against unreason-
able exactions by the Catholic clergy.[27] In 1786 the bishops

24. Burke, *Penal times,* 317.

25. Grattan-Flood, 'The diocesan manuscripts of Ferns during the rule of
Bishop Sweetman (1745-1786)', in *Archiv. Hib.* 3, 120, 123 (1914).

26. *The Good Confessor,* 115.

27. Cf. Grattan-Flood, *art. cit., Archiv. Hib.* 3, 117; MacLysaght, 'Report on
documents relating to the wardenship of Galway', in *Anal. Hib.* 14, 59;
Brady, *Eighteenth-century press,* 104 ff., 110, 174, 179, 231-2.

of Munster found it necessary to remove two parish priests for their excesses in this matter, and to warn their clergy not to be too avaricious, and especially to refrain from denouncing people from the altar. They claimed, however, that the fees fixed by law or custom could not be considered exorbitant. These were a shilling at Christmas and Easter dues, five shillings for a marriage, one-and-sixpence for a baptism, and for a funeral Mass for the dead half-a-crown to the parish priest and a shilling to the other clergy attending. There were to be no payments in goods or services.[28]

In the same year, fees on the whole somewhat higher, though with more explicit solicitude for the poor, were laid down for his diocese by the bishop of Ossory. The Christmas and Easter dues were the same as in Munster, a shilling, 'from each family that can afford it'. The maximum marriage-fee was half-a-guinea, the mean five shillings to seven-and-sixpence and nothing from 'the real poor and distressed'. For baptism, two shillings 'from such as can afford it', from 'the real poor such as they can afford or nothing', and for funeral Masses, five shillings to the parish priest and half-a-crown to the other clergy.[29]

It is only at the end of the century that a memoir based on returns made by the bishops to Castlereagh in 1801 purported to set out the material conditions of the Catholic bishops and clergy throughout the country. The income of the priests came from voluntary offerings and the dues paid at Christmas and Easter. The latter in some dioceses was a shilling from each family, in others two shillings, but the more opulent families paid varying sums up to a guinea. In some places corn was contributed – in part of co. Wexford a bushel of corn was paid yearly for every twenty acres. There were

28. Brady, *Eighteenth-century press*, 231 ff.; Renehan, *Collections*, I, 347. Here and in the following list I have given the sums in English money, though the documents give them in Irish. At the beginning of the century the ratio had been fixed at one guinea English to 22/9 Irish. Only copper Irish coins were in circulation, but the Irish reckoning was popularly used as 'money of account'.

29. Carrigan, *Ossory*, I, 193-4.

casual emoluments from marriage, churching and funerals.
The memoir summed up:

> The value of a benefice depends much on the extent of
> its population, and the degree of opulence and liberality
> of its inhabitants. The most valuable benefice is in the
> diocese of Waterford, amounting to upwards of £240
> per annum. The least valuable is in the wardenship of
> Galway, amounting to only £15 per annum. But the
> income of the parish priests generally throughout
> Ireland may be taken at an average of £65 per annum
> each, exclusively of the expense of keeping a curate . . .
> The curates . . . in most places live with their priests, who
> give them their diet and lodging, support for one horse,
> and an allowance of £10 in money . . .

On the bishops' emoluments it stated that:

> The archbishops and bishops derive their incomes, first
> from sundry parishes in their respective dioceses, which
> they hold *in commendam,* and in which generally they
> officiate as parish priests; secondly, from marriage
> licences, throughout their dioceses, and thirdly, from
> stated contributions of the parish priests and curates
> called proxies. The highest income is enjoyed by the
> Roman Catholic bishop of Cork, amounting to £550
> per annum; the lowest by the Roman Catholic bishop
> of the united dioceses of Kilfenora and Kilmacduagh,
> amounting to £100 per annum. The income of the
> several Roman Catholic bishops taken together will
> average a little more than £300 for each bishop.[30]

THE PASTORAL MISSION

The Act of 1704 (2 Anne, c.3) limited the ministrations of
the registered priest to a particular county. That of 1709

30. *Memoirs and Correspondence of Viscount Castlereagh,* IV, 97-9.

(8 Anne, c.3) restricted him to a particular parish, but did not designate any place within that area. Legally then, he might say Mass in his chapel or other suitable place, until refusal to take the Abjuration oath made the exercise of his priestly functions illegal after 25 March 1710. A draft bill of 1723 against non-juring priests shows that its framers visualized Mass being said in chapels. To facilitate identifying the celebrant it was proposed to make it illegal for a priest to say Mass in a chapel or Mass-house behind closed doors and to require him 'to appear barefaced and in public view' during the ceremony.[1] The incomplete Report of 1731[2] shows that there were in existence 892 Mass-houses, 'above one hundred . . . huts, sheds and moveable altars', and fifty-four 'private chapels' in which friars officiated. The nature of these structures varied according to the locality and the size of the Catholic population. In many places, particularly in Ulster, where most of the land was in Protestant hands and sites for Mass-houses were difficult to obtain, Mass was most commonly said in the open air. Only nine Mass-houses were recorded in the diocese of Derry in 1731, and only five in Down and Connor.[3] Outside Ulster, however, it was normal that there should be a fixed building of some kind for the celebration of Mass, though in places this could be prevented by an especially active magistrate or landlord (they were often, of course, one and the same person). In 1731 the diocese of Ferns, for example, had thirty-one Mass-houses and eleven 'moveable altars in the fields'.[4] Yet even at the height of the priestcatchers' activities Mass was said in the Dublin chapels as a matter of routine.[5]

These Mass-houses, to quote a report from Cloyne in 1731, were 'generally mean thatched cabins, many or most of them

1. Burke, *Penal times,* 458.
2. Published in *Archiv. Hib.,* vols. 1-4.
3. *Archiv. Hib.* 1, 17, 18.
4. *Ibid.* 4, 170. The diocesan statutes of 1722 (*ibid.* 27, 76-84) clearly show the bishop's anxiety to have a place where Mass, sermon and catechetical instruction could be regularly provided.
5. Cf. Donnelly, *Dublin parishes,* pt 6, 40 ff.

open at one end'.[6] From Tuam came the report that 'when a Mass-house is wanting, it is usual with some or other of the inhabitants to appoint his barn or other outhouse for the celebration of Mass'.[7] In general, the Mass was said in rude huts, sheds, or under shelters covering the altar. Although there does not appear to have been any explicit legal prohibition of the use of bells or steeples by Catholics such a ban is implicit in the exclusion from the Relief Act of 1782 of any ecclesiastic officiating in a church or chapel with a steeple or bell. Under interrogation in 1751 Bishop Sweetman of Ferns declared that his flock never rang a bell, except at the altar.[8] Of the few substantial buildings, that in Mullingar, built 'at the back of the town' in 1731, was reputed to be the only slated chapel between Dublin and Galway. It had three galleries, an altarpiece and statues.[9] Detailed descriptions of nine Dublin chapels in 1749 shows that they had galleries, paintings and pulpits. It is noted of one of them that it was the only chapel in Dublin that had no tabernacle on the altar.[10] Occasional references to accidents show that the buildings suffered from age and overcrowding.[11] Galleries appear to have been built sometimes by families and reserved exclusively for themselves to the resentment of others. In 1760 Bishop de Burgo of Ossory denounced those who demolished a gallery 'made use of for the devotion of decent people' in a Kilkenny Mass-house.[12] A gallery in Thomastown was wrecked for the third time in 1789.[13] A milder approach was made in Dublin in 1771 by asking in a

6. *Archiv. Hib.* 2, 127.

7. *Ibid.* 3, 124.

8. Burke, *Penal times*, 318.

9. *Lords' jn. Ire.*, III, 207.

10. Donnelly (ed.), *State and condition of R.C. chapels in Dublin, both secular and regular, A.D. 1749.*

11. See, for example, Donnelly, *Dublin parishes*, pt 6, 143-4; Brady, 'Some aspects of the Irish Church in the eighteenth century', in *I.E.R.* (series 5) 70, 518-9 (June 1948).

12. Carrigan, *Ossory*, I, 170.

13. Brady, *Eighteenth-century press*, 271.

newspaper why a gallery was occupied by half a dozen
people and locked while the stairs was crowded 'and room
above for near forty people'.[14] The remarks of Dr Plunkett
of Meath at his first visitation of a certain parish in 1780
throw further light on the same subject: 'the place under the
gallery is too confined and narrow to be a place of interment;
it would be meritorious for the family that turns it to that
use to sacrifice private claims of no consequence to the
wishes, health and satisfaction of the public.'[15]

Mass-houses had no legal status and during the first half
of the century their location needed careful selection. If in
a town, it was advisable to build outside the walls or in a
back street. Even a site near a public highway was a risk. A
new Mass-house at Wicklow was closed in 1702 because of
its proximity to the barracks.[16] Nearly thirty years later a
Mass-house at Great Connell was demolished because it
stood 'in the direct road' to the Protestant church.[17] For the
same reason Mass-houses were prohibited at Cloyne and
Rathluirc.[18] Chapels were closed by proclamation in 1708,
1712, 1714, 1715, 1719, 1723, 1739 and 1744, but when the
fear of invasion and internal unrest had passed they were
reopened. Otherwise they were ignored except when the
whim of some isolated landlord ordered them to be nailed
up or demolished. As late as 1781 it caused no surprise that
Lord Doneraile should 'order every Mass-house on his estate
nailed up' after he had lost a lawsuit to a parish priest,[19] and
in 1787, during the Whiteboy disturbances, it was proposed
to empower magistrates to level any chapel, in or near which
unlawful oaths were alleged to have been tendered.[20]

The experience of Dr Pococke, as narrated in his *Tour in*

14. *Ibid.,* 145.
15. Cogan, *Meath,* III, 32.
16. Burke, *Penal times,* 309.
17. *Archiv. Hib.* 4, 159.
18. *Ibid.* 2, 127.
19. Brady, *Eighteenth-century press,* 210.
20. *Ibid.,* 250-51.

Ireland in 1752,[21] was a familiar one to the traveller through Ulster. On the side of a Donegal mountain he saw several hundred people ranged around a priest who was saying Mass under a rock on an altar made of loose stones. 'For in all this country for sixty miles west, as far as Connaught, they celebrate in the open air, in the fields or on the mountains.' Within the next decade there was an improvement. In 1764 we find Archbishop Blake of Armagh being congratulated by his chapter for 'building some Mass-houses where none had been before' on account of the negligence of some parish priests.[22] A pamphlet published in the same year states:

> till within these few years, there was scarce a Mass-house to be seen in the northern counties of Ulster; now Mass-houses are spreading over most parts of that country. Convents, till of late, were hid in corners. Now they are openly avowed in the very metropolis. From the revolution till a few years ago, Mass-houses were little huts, in remote and obscure places. Now they are sumptuous buildings in the most public and conspicuous situations; as if erected to break the laws and claim establishment.[23]

The example given by the earl-bishop of Derry may not have been lost on his co-religionists. While he had no use for catholicism – 'that silly but harmless religion' – he had sympathy for the condition of Catholics. In 1788 he contemplated raising £6,000 for building cathedrals, churches and chapels for them and proposed contributing £1,000 himself for chapels in the diocese of Derry. Like most of his schemes it came to nothing; but he offered a considerable sum to Bishop M'Devitt in order 'to build a church or at least a house, so that he might not be obliged to officiate to his congregation in the open air, exposed to rain and wind'.

21. Ed. Stokes, Dublin 1891.
22. Renehan, *Collections*, I, 107.
23. *Some arguments for limiting the duration of parliament*, Dublin 1764, 5.

He gave £200 towards building a chapel in Derry, to which the corporation granted £50.[24] When a new Mass-house at Belfast was opened in 1784 the Volunteers, with other Protestants, attended Mass.[25]

In the other provinces the Mass-house was a recognized and accepted institution by about 1750. Reference has already been made to the detailed report on the Dublin chapels in 1749.[26] Both from this report and from surviving drawings and illustrations it is clear that the chapels were very unpretentious buildings, but it is clear also that by mid-century the Catholics were beginning to restore some dignity to their worship. Liffey Street chapel, for instance, is described as follows:

> This chapel though small, is neat, altar railed in, steps ascending to it of oak; fore part of the altar covered with gilt leather, and name of Jesus in glory in the midst. On the altar is a gilt tabernacle, with six large gilt candlesticks, and as many nosegays of artificial flowers. The altar piece carved and embellished with four pillars, cornices and other decorations gilt and painted. The picture of Conception of B.V.M., to whom the chapel is dedicated, fills the altar piece; and on each side are paintings of the apostles Peter and Paul. Opposite the altar hangs a handsome brass branch for tapers, near it is a neat oak pulpit, on the sounding board of which is a figure of a gilt dove, representing the descent of the Holy Ghost. In said chapel is a small sacristy, four decent confessionals, two galleries, several pews for better sort, and two sprinkling pots of black marble in chapel yard.

The chapels clustered in an area of old Dublin where Catholic churches are still thick on the ground. The parish

24. Brady, *Eighteenth-century press*, 227-8.
25. *Ibid.*, 225. After this date the newpapers report a number of instances of Protestants helping Catholics to build churches.
26. See above, note 10.

churches were in Liffey St., Mary's Lane, Arran Quay, James's St., Dirty Lane (now the upper end of Bridgefoot St.), Francis St., Cook St., Rosemary Lane and Hawkins St. The Franciscans were at Adam and Eve chapel in Cook St., the Discalced Carmelites in Wormwood Gate, the Augustinians in John's Lane, the Calced Carmelites in Ashe St. (off the Coombe), and the Capuchins in Church St. Indeed the old city seems to have become a kind of Catholic ghetto as the ascendancy moved out to the newly-built squares and more open streets. Here the Catholic printers and publishers established themselves, close to the chapels on which they depended so much for a living. Archbishop Carpenter (1770-86) lived here, at no. 20 Usher's Island. He was the first eighteenth-century archbishop of Dublin to venture a part in some kind of public and political life. What care and caution were necessary may be seen from such passing details in his correspondence as his warnings to the nuncio in Brussels, in a letter of 18 May 1776, to address all correspondence 'to a private person as follows: To Dr Carpenter, Usher's Island, Dublin'.[27] All is part of the same pattern, of a way of life rather accurately evoked by the word 'ghetto'.

In a smaller town, fairly detailed information is available for Wexford. Here the parish clergy sometimes lived uneasily with the Franciscans, for they had to share the same chapel. The chapel built within the walls by Bishop Wadding at the end of the seventeenth century had fallen down, and as the law forbade the saying of Mass within the walls of a corporate town the regular and secular clergy had to officiate in the friars' chapel, which, fortunately, was situated outside the walls. In the nature of things, disputes occurred from time to time, and these generated a correspondence which gives a detailed picture of the life of worship in Wexford town in the middle of the eighteenth century. The chapel was well equipped with vestments, linen and altar-vessels. On Sundays there were six public Masses, on weekdays three. The friars

27. Curran, 'Archbishop Carpenter's *Epistolae* (1770-1780)', in *Rep. Novum* 1, no. 2, 383 (1956).

would like to have Benediction every month, but the bishop
thought five or six times a year sufficient. Neither did he look
with favour on the stations of the Cross, erected by the
friars in 1746. One interesting reference suggests that every
evening the people may have gathered for public prayer.[28]

For the country at mid-century there are the visitation
books of Archbishop James Butler of Cashel, and an account
of a visitation of Ferns by Bishop Sweetman in 1753 which
is much briefer but more accessible and perhaps better
known.[29] Both show the same unpretentious yet decent
worship. We have descriptions of many of the chapels in
Cashel, Ballingarry for instance, in 1754:

> The chapel built due east and west, and consists of a
> stone wall seven feet high, two gable-ends, a boarded
> altar at the east end, four small windows whereof two
> are glassed; a large door in the west end with a large
> stone basin for holy water at the said door . . . well
> thatched . . .

Neither bishop gives the slightest hint that he felt any need
to cloak his activities; the visitation was carried out quite
openly, and most things were found, in the recurring phrase
of Bishop Sweetman, 'decent and well'. The precarious nature
of the toleration enjoyed is brought into sharp relief, however,
by the consideration that in 1751, only two years before
carrying out this visitation, Bishop Sweetman had been
arrested and brought to Dublin to face an interrogation with
quite unpredictable consequences, for by law he had no
right to be in the country at all.

Though the threat might never be altogether absent,
toleration was in practice effective. Old chapels were

28. Ó Súilleabháin, 'Documents relating to Wexford friary and parish,
1733-98', in *Coll. Hib.* 8, 110-28 (1965).

29. Extracts from the Cashel visitations are published by Lenihan in the
Limerick Reporter and Tipperary Vindicator, 7 Feb. 1 Aug. 1873; the Ferns
visitation is edited by Grattan-Flood, 'The diocesan manuscripts of Ferns
during the rule of Bishop Sweetman (1745-1786)', in *Archiv. Hib.* 2, 100-105
(1913).

improved and the new ones being built were slightly more
elaborate. In 1775, for example, Bishop McKenna of Cloyne
and Ross reported that in the preceding four years ten
chapels had been built and others repaired in his diocese.[30]
These church-building activities of Catholics sometimes
roused Protestant hostility. In 1764 a pamphleteer
complained:

> The truth is, they are grown so rich that they want
> power, and that they have had so much the free and
> uninterrupted exercise of their religion, that they now
> want (to use their own phrase) to give it the majesty of
> worship, nay, they are already so far advanced that
> way, that instead of having their chapels of plain and
> simple materials, and in retired places, as formerly . . .
> they now affect to have them embellished with hewn
> stone, and in the most conspicuous places they can
> pitch upon.[31]

The installation of organs, the playing of the harp at Mass,
the use of choirs, the purchase of paintings and sculpture
during the last decades of the century show a desire to have
'all the majesty of worship'; but for many years utility rather
than beauty had to be the aim of the average Catholic
church-builder, who was usually glad to have a substantial
building wherein to perform his maimed ritual. The spirit, if
not the aim, of the repressive laws had been to oblige the
Catholic to confine the external profession of his religion to
the four walls of his wretched place of worship, and the
appellation 'Mass-house' was an apt description of its main
function. Often its furnishings were restricted to the bare
essentials, and, even then, they were unfit for their purpose.

The two mid-century visitation-records mentioned above
indicate that the bishops in question sought to impose the
minimum required by decency in worship. To find more was

30. Moran, *Spicil. Ossor.*, III, 340.
31. *Advice to both the Protestants and the Papists of this kingdom: in a letter
to a great lord: and some remarks on the circumstances of each*, Dublin 1764, 9.

E

welcome, but exceptional. Both dealt summarily with anything that fell below the minimum. On 26 September 1758
Archbishop Butler makes the brusque entry: 'A stole and
ritual ordered to the flames'. Bishop Sweetman, visiting Rev.
Martin Cullen on 9 May 1753, found 'all was well except for
his purificatorium, which was torn for its dirtiness'. Bishop
Plunkett of Meath found on assuming office in 1779 that
many of the chapels were in a wretched condition, in-
adequately equipped with tattered vestments, torn altar-linen,
out-of-date missals and inferior chalices.[32] In 1790 he was
able to report that thirty-nine chapels had been rebuilt and
forty-two enlarged or repaired.[33]

Absence of fonts suggests that baptism was conferred in
private houses where marriages were also occasionally
performed or funeral Masses said. The 'station', or practice
whereby the parish priest went about to certain houses in his
often extensive parish, in order to hear confessions and
celebrate Mass at which the people of the district received
Holy Communion, also became an established practice of
Catholic life in the eighteenth century. Almost as if they were
luxuries, Archbishop Butler noted a pulpit in one chapel,
altar rails in two and tabernacles in two more (though in
Dublin there was only one chapel lacking a tabernacle). In
three parishes he found blue vestments, gifts perhaps from
Irish in Spain. In 1788 the bishop of Ossory noted in one
parish 'a blue v[estmen]t sint from Spain'.[34] From the
absence of any mention of a monstrance in fragmentary lists
of furnishings of churches in Cashel and Ossory it would
seem that Benediction was given only when the bishop came
on visitation. In 1780, outlining the order followed by him
on such occasions, the archbishop of Cashel stated that he
ended the visitation with Benediction 'which gave me an
opportunity of speaking on the real presence'. A list of the
pontificalia of Ossory in 1787 included 'a small silver re-

32. See the detailed account of his 1780 visitation in Cogan, *Meath*, III, 25-44.
33. *Ibid.*, III, 136.
34. Carrigan, *Ossory*, I, 205.

monstrance for the visitations, with a case, made by sub-scriptions of the diocesan clergy'.[35] Four years later, the bishop of Cloyne willed to the chapels of Cove and Ballymore 'the ornaments for the Benediction of the Blessed Sacrament'.[36] In 1775 he had reported that benediction was given monthly and on more solemn occasions in five places in his diocese.[37]

In a *relatio* of 1790 Dr Plunkett of Meath told how, because of the penal laws, Catholic worship had been stripped of all external solemnity, but how there had been a revival and an effort to spread the splendour of public worship since the Relief Act of 1782.[38] During the next few years this was evident to Catholics and Protestants. In Dublin in 1787 numerous Protestant nobility and laity attended a pontifical High Mass. The music for the ceremony was composed by Tommaso Giordani, the music director of Francis St. chapel, and was accompanied by an orchestra.[39] When a charity sermon for schools was preached in Limerick in 1793, the bishop wrote that his chapel 'was brim full of Protestants, clergy and laity' and music was played 'by a fine band of music, mostly gentlemen'.[40] A like congregation attended a solemn requiem at Cork, in the same year, for Louis XVI.[41]

The importance of the Mass-house was, of course, that it made Mass available to the people in a public place and at a fixed hour. Archbishop Blake of Armagh, we have seen already, had been very assiduous in building Mass-houses in his diocese. He was also insistent that Mass be said at a convenient time, and that the Sunday Mass especially should not be removed from 'the usual station'.[42] Martin Marley, himself an Irish priest, has an interesting passage in his *Good*

35. *Ibid.,* I, 196.
36. Carrigan, 'Catholic episcopal wills: Cashel', in *Archiv. Hib.* 3, 176 (1914).
37. Moran, *Spicil. Ossor.,* III, 340.
38. Cogan, *Meath,* III, 138-9.
39. Brady, *Eighteenth-century press,* 287.
40. Conway, 'Correspondence of Dr. Bray', in *Archiv. Hib.* 1, 225 (1912).
41. Brady, *Eighteenth-century press,* 287.
42. Renehan, *Collections,* I, 105-6.

Confessor, the pastoral handbook which he published in 1743, which assumes the obligation of the parish priest to provide his parishioners with Mass at a fixed time and place. The form for the examination of conscience which he sets for the use of parish priests runs in part as follows:

> Did you ever give your parishioners time and opportunity to offer themselves to confessions, Sundays and Holy-days? Have you appointed a fixt hour for saying Mass at both stations? . . . Have you said Mass in your stations at the time appointed or thereabouts? . . . Did you remove the parish Mass from the usual station on Sundays or Holy-days? How many did you think lost Mass for that removal?[43]

Provincial and diocesan statutes stressed the obligation imposed on parish priests by the Council of Trent to preach and instruct on Sundays and holydays. Full use was made of the weekly meeting between priest and people as an opportunity of instruction and devotion. *The Good Confessor* speaks of an hour as the normal time for Mass and sermon: 'if a pastor appoints to say his first Mass, suppose at nine, I give him to ten to say Mass and catechize his flock'. He also speaks of those who, inevitably, were reluctant to preach: 'what will become of the unhappy pastors who do not catechize ten times in the year, no, not once in ten years . . . and what shall we say of their confessors?'[44] In Cashel and Ferns we find the bishop on visitation enquiring very diligently as to whether the Sunday sermon is given regularly. 'The chapel is duly served on festivals with Mass, sermon, exhortation, prone or catechism', Archbishop Butler notes; in another place he says of the parish priest: 'he has the constitutions and prone of the diocese . . . he prones and exhorts very often'. Bishop Sweetman too comments from time to time on the pastor's preaching, though more normally

43. *The Good Confessor,* 112-13.
44. *Ibid.,* 110-13.

he notes only those who are failing in this duty, like John Fitzhenry, fascinatingly noted as 'an honest, indolent man, who neither preaches nor teaches his flock'. It is clear that the bishop and his vicar general keep a watchful eye on delinquents, though in some cases they find it hard to bring about an improvement; the Cashel visitation books make it very clear indeed that any priest found without 'the constitutions, prone and catechism of the diocese' got only a few days to produce them personally to the archbishop in Thurles.[45]

On occasions like the episcopal visitation the people would hear a sermon from the bishop or some special preacher. At times too they might be addressed by friars conducting some kind of rudimentary and unorganized mission, though there is evidence that such visitors were not always welcome to the parish priest, who at times might have reasons for being inhospitable (again I quote from *The Good Confessor,* written, it will be remembered, by a parish priest):

> Did you hinder preachers or missioners to exhort your flock to advance the glory of God, though you have exhorted them yourself at due times (except vagabonds, who go about to preach purely for lucre, and are of an irregular life?).[46]

It was seldom, however, that the people heard any preacher apart from their own priest, who, no doubt, often relied on the 'prone of the diocese', the book of set sermons insisted on in many diocesan statutes. Of course a sermon of this kind was not necessarily less effective than one composed by the priest himself, but the 'prone' was usually a continental production, 'in Latin or French or other languages . . . but generally in a style not so well adapted to our country', as Bishop Gallagher of Raphoe wrote in 1736 in the preface to his *Sixteen Irish sermons, in an easy and familiar stile,* the only devotional book in Irish, apart from catechisms, to be

45. See above, note 29.
46. *The Good Confessor,* 98.

published in Ireland in the eighteenth century. It had an enormous success, due largely, no doubt, to its real merits, but also indicating the greatness of the need it met.

Statutes for the diocese of Cork enacted in 1768[47] require a preacher to be prepared with knowledge derived from study and meditation. He should not talk over the heads of his people, he should avoid levity, apocryphal stories, un-authentic miracles, or the prediction of future events. 'The gospel and epistle of the day and the particular abuses of the parish, will always furnish abundant matters of familiar exhortation' were the visitation remarks of Dr Plunkett of Meath in 1780. 'Were I to say but three words, I would turn about to the people every Sunday and holyday and would say these three words.'[48]

Sometimes the Sunday instruction took the form of teaching the catechism, though documents such as Arch-bishop Butler's visitation at mid-century and Clogher diocesan statutes of 1789[49] indicate that this task was usually delegated to the schoolmaster or the young man preparing for holy orders. In each parish, Archbishop Butler enquires carefully about the schoolmasters, and especially if they teach the catechism. His procedure with those who do not teach it shows that he regarded teaching catechism as part of the schoolmaster's duty – in one parish, for example, we find a schoolmaster who is 'ordered to teach the Christian doctrine', and in another two 'to be reproved for neglect in teaching the catechism'.

As early as 1726 there is reference to another source of Sunday instruction. The catechism of Dr Michael Blake, which was in circulation in both English and Irish from about 1726, contains 'an abridgement of the faith to be said on Sundays at the parish Mass, and in private families'. Presumably it was read aloud to the congregation. This practice became very widespread after 1772, when Clement

47. *Statuta synodalia pro dioecesi Corcagiensi,* Cork 1768.
48. Cogan, *Meath,* III, 31.
49. *Archiv. Hib.* 12, 62-9 (1946).

XIV extended to Ireland the indulgence for the recitation of these prayers before Mass. Archbishop Carpenter's *Ritual*, published in 1776, gives an elaborate list of prayers, in English and Irish, the latter in a translation by Charles O'Conor. Before Mass the priest read to the assembled people an exhortation, the commandments of God and of the Church, the sacraments, and the acts of contrition, faith, hope and charity, preceded by a special 'prayer before the acts'.[50] This practice has only recently ceased to be a feature of public worship in Ireland. Another practice, even more distinctively Irish, was the recital of the psalm *De profundis* after the last Gospel. This had become an established custom at the beginning of the eighteenth century, and was discontinued only in November 1960.

Legislation directed against the number of Catholic holydays observed in Ireland was enacted in 1695 by the Williamite parliament (7 Will. III, c. 14). It imposed a fine of two shillings, and in default of payment, the punishment of whipping, on labourers and servants who refused to work on any day that was not a Sunday or statutory holyday. Twenty-nine traditional holydays, of which St Patrick's day was not one, were retained by the statute. A proclamation in 1707 commanded that 'no Popish priest . . . presume to publish any such holyday at Mass', if it were not a statutory one, and directed all magistrates to enforce the provisions of the 1695 Act.[51] Though there were to be a number of complaints that the many holydays the Irish were forced to observe were 'a great occasion of their idleness and poverty', the very complaints are an indication that no consistent attempt was made to enforce the Act of 1695.

At the request of the Irish bishops, Pope Benedict XIV, in December 1755, reduced the holydays of obligation to the Nativity, Circumcision, Epiphany, Ascension, Corpus Christi, Mondays after Easter and Whit, the Purification, the

---

50. Hawkes, 'Irish form of preparation for Sunday Mass in the eighteenth century', in *Rep. Novum* 1, no. 1, 183-92 (1955); Wall, 'Archbishop John Carpenter and the Catholic revival, 1770-1786', *ibid.*, 177-8.

51. Brady, *Eighteenth-century press*, 7-8.

Annunciation, the Assumption and the Nativity of Our Lady, the feasts of saints Patrick, Stephen, John the Baptist, Peter and Paul and of All Saints. This meant that nineteen holydays had been abolished, or, more accurately, abolished in part, for on these days the Pope removed only the obligation of abstaining from servile work. The obligation of hearing Mass remained.[52] It was many times represented to the Holy See that is was very difficult for poor day-labourers to hear Mass before beginning their day's work, and over the years several dioceses were released from this obligation of hearing Mass on a retrenched holyday.[53] Finally, in 1778, Pius VI abolished this obligation for the whole country, and further shortened the list of holydays by removing the feast of St Stephen and three feasts of Our Lady, the Purification, Nativity and Immaculate Conception. These three feasts, however, continued to be observed in some dioceses well into the nineteenth century.[54]

After the Mass, the most marked devotion among Irish penal-day Catholics was to Our Lady. Piaras Mac Gearailt, forced to conform because of economic pressure, found the absence of devotion to Mary the most distasteful aspect of 'the Saxon Lutheran religion'. The description of the Dublin chapels in 1749

> preserves for us much evidence of the strong devotion to Our Lady which was practised in these makeshift buildings. In Liffey Street, there was a picture of the Immaculate Conception, in Francis Street, of the Assumption. In Cooke Street (St Audoen's parish) a statue of the Blessed Virgin with a diadem on her head, the infant Jesus on one arm and a sceptre on the opposite hand stood between the pulpit and the sacristy. The Franciscans in Adam and Eve's had as an altarpiece

52. Renehan, *Collections*, I, 317–18.
53. Moran, *Spicil. Ossor.*, III, 322, 383; Curran, 'Archbishop Carpenter's *Epistolae* (1770-1780)', in *Rep. Novum* 1, no. 1, 159 (1955); 'Correspondence of Archbishop Carpenter with Bishop Sweetman of Ferns', *ibid.*, no. 2, 400.
54. Renehan, *Collections*, I, 318.

a large painting of 'the Crucifixion and of the Assumption and Annunciation', while the Dominicans in Bridge Street had pictures of the Assumption and of St Dominic receiving the Rosary from Our Lady and the nearby Carmelites in Wormwood Gate had a representation of Our Lady giving the scapular to St Simon Stock.[55]

Of all the Marian devotions, the rosary had pride of place with both clergy and laity. An instruction to the clergy of Clonfert in 1725 directs that 'the clergy, both secular and regular, will in the beginning of their Masses say their beads *in lingua vulgari* on Sundays and holydays, and in every family prayers at night'.[56] 'The beads is duly observed by most of the people' notes Archbishop Butler on visitation of Borris parish in 1759. Next year he noted that the schoolmaster of Killenaule 'teaches the beads in the chapel before Mass on Sundays'. In Protestant eyes the rosary was indeed a kind of talisman of Popery and Jacobitism – when the Young Pretender was burnt in effigy at Youghal in October 1745 he had 'a bundle of rosaries (or padareens) hung to his nose, to show his obedience to the Pope'.[57]

Finally, a few words may be said on Catholic education, emphasizing in particular how closely the schoolmaster worked with the priest as a teacher of religion. (That he taught religion was undoubtedly one important reason why he was proscribed. Like the priest, however, the law was not effectively invoked against him.) As early as 1730 the diocesan statutes of Dublin oblige every priest with the care of souls to have in his parish a schoolmaster to teach the Christian doctrine.[58] It seems, however, that it was the establishment of the Charter schools by Archbishop Boulter in 1733 which led the Catholic bishops to give serious thought to setting up

55. Meagher, 'Glimpses of eighteenth-century priests', in *Rep. Novum* 2, no. 1, 130 (1957-8).
56. Burke, *Penal times,* 251.
57. Brady, *Eighteenth-century press,* 72-3.
58. Moran, *Spicil. Ossor.,* III, 139.

schools. It has already been noted that the Charter schools
were perhaps the main factor in the Irish initiative of 1738
which led to the far-reaching reorganization of the pastoral
mission in 1751.[59] John Kent, in his report of 1742, clearly
considered them a serious threat. He suggested it might be
met by a greater commitment of the clergy, especially the
religious, to catechetical instruction.[60] In 1743 and 1744 a
further exchange of views with the congregation of Propaganda led to more ambitious plans being drawn up to
counter it. The bishops were to be helped to set up schools
in the principal towns, the Irish lay Catholics were to be
urged to lend their support, and hopes were expressed that
the regular clergy would also help by setting up their own
schools.[61]

All this had to be done very quietly, especially after the
political crisis in 1745. Nevertheless, when the four archbishops sent Fr John Murphy to Rome in 1750 he was able
to report that there were 1,400 Catholic children in the
schools which had been set up, 400 boys in Dublin alone,
with 200 others apprenticed to trades. The education of
girls was being looked after by the nuns. Money was being
collected in Ireland, but more was urgently needed. Catholic
Europe would have to help. Propaganda agreed to pay an
annual subsidy to the Catholic schools in Ireland.[62] The
amount was small – the annual share of the diocese of
Ferns,[63] for example, was between £7 and £8 – but every help
was welcome.

In the 1750s, as has been seen, the parish schoolmaster was
an established institution in the diocese of Cashel. Writing
to Propaganda in 1772 Archbishop Carpenter of Dublin
says that with the Roman subsidy and money scraped

59. See above, p. 39.

60. *Archiv. Hib.* 28, 90 ff. (1966).

61. MacFhinn, 'Scríbhinní i gCartlainn an Vatican', in *Anal. Hib.* 16, 167-9
(1946); Wall, *The Penal Laws,* 11-12.

62. MacFhinn, *loc. cit., Anal. Hib.* 16, 173 ff., 182-3.

63. Cf. Curran, 'Correspondence of Archbishop Carpenter with Bishop
Sweetman of Ferns', in *Rep. Novum* 1, no. 2, 399-405 (1956).

together in various ways he has made himself personally responsible for the schooling of more than 160 boys, besides those he has caused to be apprenticed to trades (the repeated juxtaposition of 'school' and 'apprenticeship' shows how consciously the Catholic effort was in answer to the Charter schools, whose parliamentary grant had been substantially increased after 1757). Many other schools, the archbishop said, were maintained by the generosity of the wealthier Catholics, but the position of these was essentially a precarious one.[64] Nevertheless, five or six years after the Relief Act of 1782 had given Catholics legal permission to teach provided they took the oath of allegiance and were licensed by the Protestant bishop, forty-seven Catholic schools existed in Dublin, with nearly 1,800 pupils. In most cases, phrases such as 'popish charity school connected with the popish chapel' or 'supported by annual subscription and charity sermon' make it clear that they are parish schools.[65]

THE RELIGIOUS MIND

The rise of the Catholic printers and booksellers was one of the most remarkable developments of the penal days. The eighteenth-century code contained no fresh legislation against them, but statutes of Edward VI and James I would have been sufficient proscription if they had been put into effect. Yet from the very beginning of the century sporadic protests and seizures indicate that Catholic books were being printed in Ireland as well as being imported from the continent.[1] As was the case with so many other aspects of Catholic life, printers and booksellers soon came to enjoy a

64. Archbishop Carpenter to the cardinal prefect of Propaganda, 20 May 1772, Moran, *Spicil. Ossor.,* III, 324-6. See also the archbishop's *Relatio Status* of 1780, ed. Curran in *Rep. Novum* 1, no. 2, 396 (1956).

65. Brady, 'Catholic schools in Dublin in 1787–8', in *Rep. Novum* 1, no. 1, 193-6 (1955).

1. Cf. Brady, *Eighteenth-century press,* 10, 42, 50; Meagher, 'Glimpses of eighteenth-century priests', in *Rep. Novum* 2, no. 1, 130 ff. (1957-8).

practical toleration. Most of them, naturally, were in Dublin, but there were printers in the larger provincial centres also, and most towns had a Catholic bookseller, even though the sale of books was usually only part of his business. During the penal days the Irish Catholics became a reading people in a quite new way, and a glance at the booksellers' trade provides an insight into their religious life which is not available for earlier periods.

What did they read? One approach to this question is to study the booksellers' lists and to note the works most constantly on offer. Yet a book may be a perennial on such lists either because it is selling well or because it is scarcely selling at all, and it is necessary to apply a control by taking into account the number of Irish printings of any particular book. Marley's *The Good Confessor*, for instance, is on very many lists, yet it never had a Dublin printing. Certain books, however, are clearly established favourites. To note only the more striking, there is the translation by Thomas Hawkins of *The Holy Court* by the French Jesuit, Nicholas Caussin, chaplain to Louis XIII; Darrell, the English Jesuit, especially his *Moral Reflections on the Epistles and Gospels of every Sunday throughout the year;* Fleury's *Historical Catechism;* Robert Manning's *Moral Entertainments* and controversial works; *The Poor Man's Catechism* by John Anselm Mannock, O.S.B.; *An Essay on the Rosary* by the Irish Dominican, John O'Connor; Parsons' *Christian Directory;* and the *Introduction to the Devout Life* by St Francis de Sales.[2]

Beyond question, however, the most popular spiritual author in eighteenth-century Ireland was Richard Challoner, both in his translation of *The Imitation of Christ*, and in his own works, *The Garden of the Soul, Think Well On't* and *Meditations for every day of the year*.[3] His popularity only serves to emphasize what must already be apparent from the

---

2. Cf. Wall, *The sign of Doctor Hay's Head,* 71-90; Ó Súilleabháin, 'Catholic sermon-books printed in Ireland, 1700-1850)' in *I.E.R.* (series 5) 99, 31-36 (Jan. 1963); 'Clódóireacht Chaitliceach in Éireann san ochtú haois déag', in *Irisleabhar Muighe Nuadhat* 1964, 95-101.

3. Wall, *op. cit.,* 75-7.

list given above – how little of this literature was of native origin. The *Essay on the Rosary* is the only Irish work in the list of selected 'best-sellers', and while the selection must be to some degree arbitrary, in this respect the general proportions are not unfairly preserved.

However, before accusing the Dublin printers of neglecting Irish spirituality by being too eager to push their trade it is necessary to attempt some assessment of that considerable section of the people whose devotional reading was in Irish. As already noted, the only devotional book in Irish printed during the period was Bishop Gallagher's *Sixteen Irish Sermons, in an easy and familiar stile* in 1736. In these sermons, the bishop deliberately forsook the antiquated style of literary Irish for the simpler popular language. His great success was sufficient indication of the need for such a departure, but there were none to follow him.

In the absence of printed editions, the relative popularity of devotional works in Irish is best tested by considering the numbers of surviving manuscripts – the most popular texts were those which were copied and re-copied. By this test the most popular works were the *Meditationes Vitae Christi* attributed to St Bonaventure; Mac Aingil's *Scáthán Shacramuinte na hAithridhe;* Gearnon's *Parrthas an anma;* Keating's *Eochair-sgiath an Aifrinn* and *Tri bior-ghaoithe an bháis;* and *Saltair Mhuire,* a tract on the rosary. Two further works may be added to the list, *An Sgáthan Spioradálta,* a translation of Angelo Elli's *Lo specchio spirituale del principio e fine della vita humana,* made by the Franciscan Thomas McGauran in the seventeenth century, and *Trompa na bhFlaitheas,* a 1755 translation of Antoine Yvan's *La trompette du ciel* (no eighteenth-century manuscript of this is extant, but its popularity is attested by a number of early nineteenth-century manuscripts).[4]

Again, these works can hardly be considered as best suited to serve popular Irish spirituality in the eighteenth century.

4. I am indebted to Pádraig Ó Súilleabháin, O.F.M., for the information in this paragraph, and also for many valuable suggestions on the whole question of Catholic printing in the eighteenth century.

The translations are again in evidence, but even more striking is the failure to use the printing-press, which must be put down to the conservative character of the Irish literary tradition. Some of these works which were multiplied in manuscript had already been printed over a century before at Louvain and other continental centres, and while an author like Mac Aingil had in his day made a conscious attempt to break with the pedantries of the literary tradition and cultivate what he modestly called 'simple style and poor writing', further simplification and development was needed by the eighteenth century, and in this, as already noted, Bishop Gallagher found no followers.

'In the Irish as well as the English books,' Dr Wall writes, 'it is vain to look for any of the indigenous pieties and observances of the Irish countryside of the period, the pilgrimages and patterns and visits at the ancient holy wells.'[5] It was of course only to be expected that the government should look askance at such practices. Quite apart from any religious aspect they might have, the occasion which they gave for assemblies of Catholics could be considered a political danger. Legislation of 1703 (2 Anne, c. 6, 27) forbade all pilgrimages, mentioning St Patrick's Purgatory by name, and imposed a fine of ten shillings on each person apprehended, half to go to the discoverer, half to the poor of the parish. The penalty of a public whipping was imposed in default of payment. All who set up booths in such places to sell ale or victuals were to be fined twenty shillings, and the magistrates were ordered to 'demolish all crosses, pictures and inscriptions that are anywhere publickly set up and are the occasion of popish superstitions'.

Like so much of the penal code, this law was enforced only very sporadically. There is evidence of the suppression of pilgrimages for a time, particularly in the vicinity of Dublin, as at St John's Well in County Meath in 1710 or at Glendalough in 1714.[6] In later years the local magistrates occasion-

5. *The sign of Dr Hay's Head,* 106.
6. Brady, *Eighteenth-century press,* 14; Burke, *Penal times,* 310; Walsh, 'Glimpses of the penal times', in *I.E.R.* (series 4) 29, 137-9 (Feb. 1911).

ally took action, but in general the pilgrimages continued. St Patrick's Purgatory, though mentioned by name in the statute, was never interfered with. A number of detailed descriptions of the pilgrimage in penal days have been preserved, many of them from Protestants.[7] The *turas Locha Deirg* seems to have been commonly imposed as a penalty for grave sin, and the great pilgrimage-centre continued to flourish.

There is ample evidence, however, to show that these pilgrimages and other traditional religious practices, especially patterns and wakes, met with a great deal of ecclesiastical disapproval, because they were the occasion of serious superstitions. Superstitions were not, of course, confined to such practices. *The Good Confessor* gives a long list on which he feels his penitents might profitably make examination of conscience:

> Did you make use of any superstitions, or vain observations, persuading yourself that there are lucky and unlucky days: unlucky, if the first person you should meet in the morning should be red-haired, or if a hare should cross the way before you, or if a grave should be opened on a Tuesday, or if a marriage, or any bargain should be made on that day of the week, upon which Holy Innocents fell that year, or if thirteen should be at table etc., which are the remains of heathenism, vain and groundless remarks.
> Did you make use of superstitious things for curing of diseases in men or cattle, which have, or can have, no natural connection with these effects, such as billets, certain words, prayers not approved by the Church, herbs gathered before sunrise, or on certain days only, a

7. There is a detailed description from Bishop MacMahon of Clogher in 1714 (Moran, *Spicil. Ossor.*, II, 479-80). See also Nary, *Brief History of St Patrick's Purgatory* (1718); Hewson, *A description of St Patrick's Purgatory in Lough Derg; and an account of the pilgrim's business there* (1727); Richardson, *The great folly, superstition and idolatry of pilgrimages in Ireland* (1727); *Gentleman's Magazine*, Feb. 1766, in Brady, *Eighteenth-century press*, 118-21.

little stone, or flint-arrow dipped in milk, ale or water . . .
had you recourse to magicians, sorcerers, or witches?[8]

Yet it seems beyond doubt that pilgrimages, wakes and
patterns were the most serious occasions of superstition, and
that they became much worse in this respect as the century
advanced.[9] While denunciations might be expected from such
writers as the author of *The Good Confessor*, who admits that
he might be accused of belonging to the 'Jansenistic' or
'rigoristic' school, they came too from quarters which might
have been expected to be more sympathetic. Bishop Gallagher
of Raphoe, for example, after his transfer to Kildare and
Leighlin, condemned the custom of keening at funerals and
'the unchristian diversions of lewd songs, of brutal tricks
called fronsy-fronsy' at wakes, and threatened persistent
offenders with excommunication.[10]

For the whole of the penal period, then, the bishops found
it necessary to set themselves against superstitious usages.
Archbishop Butler of Cashel made an enquiry on this point
as part of the regular visitation of a parish, though he was
usually able to record 'no necromancers, no fairy men or
women or superstitious actions'. There can be little doubt
that such constant vigilance was called for, and it is also
probably true to say that ecclesiastical authority would have
been content to see that the faith was not contaminated by
superstitious usages in connection with wakes, patterns and
pilgrimages. For instance, the bishop of Ferns in 1771 and
his neighbour of Ossory in 1782 forbade their priests to
celebrate Mass on the actual site where a pattern was held.
Mass was to be celebrated in public on such an occasion
only if the day was a Sunday or holyday, and it should be
celebrated in the nearest chapel. No doubt this was a
necessary precaution, both because of the superstitions

8. *The Good Confessor*, 73.

9. Cf. Moran, *Spicil. Ossor.*, III, 143-4, 379, 393; Brady, *Eighteenth-century
press*, 85, 115, 186, 256; Renehan, *Collections*, I, 105, 479; Carrigan, *Ossory*, I,
170.

10 *The Good Confessor*, 45, 53, 92; Comerford, *Kildare and Leighlin*, I, 81-2.

associated with these practices, and also because it seems abundantly clear that by this date patterns had become, in the words of Bishop Sweetman, 'meetings of pretended devotion, or rather of real dissipation and dissoluteness' and not of genuine religious observance.[11] One might nevertheless ask the question – which, of course, historical investigation cannot answer – if this deterioration was caused by an over-rigoristic approach on the part of ecclesiastical authority, which inclined it to meet the real problems connected with these traditional religious observances by denunciation and suppression rather than by sympathetic direction.

One notable step was however taken in the middle of the eighteenth century to revive the liturgical cult of the Irish saints.[12] Since the counter-reformation the missal and breviary of Pope Pius V had come into general use, and these made no provision for any local cults. In the seventeenth century the efforts of Luke Wadding, O.F.M., had given St Patrick a place in the Roman breviary and missal. Now steps were taken to secure approval for a special Irish supplement to the liturgical books. The Irish bishops presented a petition for the cult in Ireland and in the Irish colleges abroad of Pope Celestine I and nine Irish saints, Malachy, Laurence O'Toole, Brigid, Columba, Columbanus, Gall, Frigidian, Rumold and Dympna. Pope Benedict XIV gave his approval on 8 July 1741. All the saints on the list, it may be noted, already had a well-attested liturgical cult, though as a matter of history it can be at least seriously questioned if the last three were in fact Irish. In 1745 Thomas de Burgo, O.P., received a further commission from the bishops to seek approval of the cult of fourteen additional saints. Some of these also had a well-attested cult on the continent (again there are the same historical doubts as to whether all were in fact Irish), and there was no difficulty in extending their cult to Ireland. For others no evidence of

11. Grattan-Flood, 'The diocesan manuscripts of Ferns during the rule of Bishop Sweetman (1745-1786)', in *Archiv. Hib.* 3, 118 (1914); Brady, *Eighteenth-century press*, 186; Moran, *Spicil. Ossor.*, III, 379.

12. Cf. Carrigan, *Ossory*, I, 159-61.

F

cult could be found in accepted liturgical books. However, it was decided in 1747 to allow the cult of all fourteen saints in Ireland, provided that in each case any special Mass or historical lessons for the breviary should be taken from books already approved. If no such proper texts could be found, the Mass and office were to be taken from the common.

In 1751 de Burgo published in Dublin the *officia propria* of the twenty-four saints, all with proper historical lessons, which he had composed himself in those cases where he could find none already approved. His publication did not win acceptance in Ireland because it did not follow the instructions of the Roman decree of 1747, and this delayed the use of the new offices by the Irish clergy, possibly until 1769, when an edition of the *officia propria* conforming exactly to Roman requirements was printed in Paris.

De Burgo's 1751 edition may also have handicapped attempts to secure approbation of the cult of other Irish saints, especially of the diocesan patrons, with which Archbishop Carpenter of Dublin was particularly associated in the early 1770s. The diocesan patrons would in any case have caused difficulty in Rome, for they were not to be found in any approved liturgical books, some of them not even being in the Roman Martyrology. Neither were Irish historical studies sufficiently advanced to produce an account of them which might hope to win Roman approval, though in fact Archbishop Carpenter was associated with the new beginning of such studies in Dublin.[13] He did not, however, succeed in getting approbation for any more Irish saints, though in 1777 he had an edition of the Roman Missal published in Dublin, complete with Irish supplement, in order to popularize further the cult of those saints who had been approved.

It seems beyond doubt that the main influence working towards new directions in Irish Catholic spirituality in the penal times was the religious literature published in English.

13. Curran, 'Archbishop Carpenter's *Epistolae* (1770-1780)' in *Rep. Novum* 1, no. 1, 158 ff. (1955); Wall, 'Archbishop John Carpenter and the Catholic revival', *ibid.,* 179-82.

The Irish language had entered its long defensive, and the age-old religious practices met with scant encouragement. It must be remembered, of course, that this literature coming from the Dublin printing-houses influenced directly only a minority. No attempt has yet been made at any kind of exact analysis of the reading public for these works, though no doubt patient work on the lists of subscribers they so often include should yield valuable information. Passing references indicate that as their life became more secure the clergy developed habits of reading. The published wills of the eighteenth-century bishops show how episcopal libraries grew from small beginnings in the worst days at the beginning of the century – Bishop Armstrong of Down and Connor, who died in 1739, left effects valued at £60. 12., of which the most important single item, apart from £10. 10. 6. cash, was books valued at £8[14] – to the 4000 volumes left by Archbishop Carpenter in 1786.[15] Information about priests' libraries is not so easy to come by. The statement in the will of Dr Nary (1738) that 'most of my worldly substance consists of my library'[16] can hardly be regarded as typical, for we should have known this from his scholar's life in any case, but when, for example, we find a bishop putting his name down for fifty or sixty copies of a book it is a fair inference that he meant them for the priests of his diocese, though the lack of exact research into subscribers' lists means that here too one can only record passing impressions.[17] Again, it is necessary to take account of the fact that so many of the clergy were educated in France. The 'prone of the diocese', on Bishop Gallagher's testimony, was more often in French or Latin, but this need not exclude a considerable reliance on English books in the actual preparation of the sermon. John Wickham, parish priest of Templeshannon and

14. Carrigan, 'Catholic episcopal wills: Armagh', in *Archiv. Hib.* 1, 168-9 (1912).

15. Wall, *The sign of Doctor Hay's Head,* 115-16.

16. Donnelly, *Dublin parishes,* pt 10, 55.

17. Cf. Ó Súilleabháin, 'Catholic books printed in Ireland 1740-1820 containing subscribers' lists', in *Coll. Hib.* 6-7, 231-3 (1963-4).

Edermine in the diocese of Ferns, had been educated in Louvain. His library of some 260 volumes passed to the Wexford Franciscans on his death in 1777. It was well stocked with sermon material in French, ranging from the workaday prone to classical authors like Bourdaloue and Bossuet, and the overall number of French books would suggest that he retained a reasonable command of the language. Yet an examination of the books themselves, now in the Franciscan Library, Killiney, gives some indications that it was to English sources he was inclined to turn for his own Sunday sermon.[18]

It is very difficult, of course, to offer an assessment of what the mass of the people read for themselves. Their reading may very well have been largely confined to the chap-book lives of the saints hawked around the country by travelling pedlars, together with secular writings of a not dissimilar type such as *The Irish Rogues and Rapparees, The Life and Adventures of Captain Freney, The Battle of Aughrim,* and so forth.[19] In this matter of popular reading the Irish-language tradition may well have been more respectable, with the solider works reaching further down the social scale among a people not yet dependent on the printed book. It would, however, seem safe to suggest that the bulk of the people depended for their spiritual formation on the Sunday instruction and the catechism.

There is no definitive survey of eighteenth-century catechisms, particularly of those in the English language, but one might venture the opinion that it is unlikely that such a survey would disturb the pattern which at this stage seems to be suggesting itself. In trying to assess the forces which formed the Irish spirituality which emerged from the penal period it seems that very considerable weight must be given to the devotional works which were printed in such great numbers in Ireland. This in turn suggests that the epithet 'Jansenistic' which has been so freely applied to certain

18. Ó Súilleabháin, 'The library of a parish priest of the penal days', *ibid.,* 234-44.
19. Wall, *The sign of Doctor Hay's Head,* 109 ff.

salient characteristics of this spirituality may have been used
without sufficient consideration.

Early in the century the nuncio in Brussels put considerable
pressure on the Irish bishops to declare their formal acceptance of the bull *Unigenitus,* because he had reason to fear
Jansenist penetration in Ireland, but it seems that the only
real substance for these fears was the fact that Bishop Fagan
of Meath had ordained a number of priests on dimissorial
letters from the Jansenist chapter of Utrecht. It seems equally
certain that Bishop Fagan had performed these ordinations
through a failure to appreciate the issues at stake rather than
through any attachment to Jansenism, and there is no
doubt whatsoever that the reason for the reluctance of the
Irish bishops to obey the nuncio's commands was a fear of
the political and legal consequences they might incur, at a
time when the penal code was still rigorously enforced, if it
became known that they had formally acknowledged the
acceptance of papal legislation in Ireland. There is no reason
to question their assurances to the nuncio that in Ireland
neither bishops, priests nor people accepted the teachings of
Jansenism. Dr Ruth Clark has assembled impressive
evidence from which she concludes that the Irish in Paris with
hardly an exception throughout the eighteenth century were
to be found on the side of the bull *Unigenitus,* that the Irish
college in Paris was a well-known centre of orthodoxy, and
that its orthodoxy was closely connected with the general
orthodoxy of Ireland on the Jansenist question.[20]

Something of a crisis seems to have developed on this
issue in the early 1730s. It arose from the fact that one of the
Irish bishops, Dr Dunne of Kildare and Leighlin, had given
the Roman authorities cause to suspect him of Jansenism.
The available documentation is too incomplete to assess the
merits of his case with any real finality, but a few interesting
points emerge from it. One is that the nuncio in Brussels
reported that Jansenist ideas were held by only a very few

20. Clark, *Strangers and sojourners at Port Royal,* 210–19. For the crisis in
Ireland early in the century see Giblin, 'Catalogue Nunz. di Fiandra', in
Coll. Hib. 5, 73-4, 81-9, 104 (1962).

people in Ireland, and that before this particular incident there had been no Jansenism at all. On the same occasion, one of the superiors of the Irish Lombard college in Paris felt it necessary to call attention to the institution's well-known anti-Jansenist record, and in the course of his remarks he said that the Roman-trained priests, for unworthy motives, were far too free in stigmatizing the Paris priests as 'Jansenists'. It is true that on a number of occasions the Irish regulars complained to Rome that some of the seculars were imbued with 'French ideas', though in so far as these were particularized they seem to have been Gallican rather than Jansenist. A pattern does seem to emerge which is hardly straining the evidence. At the time, relations between the secular and regular clergy were bad. The continental background of most of the regulars was Roman, while that of most of the seculars was French. In their disputes, the words 'Gallican' and 'Jansenist' seem to have been used fairly freely by the regulars to discredit the seculars in Rome. In some cases, there may have been a certain foundation for a charge of Gallicanism, but on the testimony of the Brussels nuncio – and few could have been better informed – there was little or none for a charge of Jansenism.[21]

Even in France, Jansenism had by this date in the eighteenth century become an essentially political issue: it is hard to attach to the term a religious significance more precise than that of a general tendency towards a stern morality. It does not follow, of course, that any tendency to take the stern view in moral matters must be traced to a Jansenist source, and from what has been said it must be clear that any

21. See Fenning, 'Some problems of the Irish mission, 1733-1774', in *Coll. Hib.* 8, 60 ff. (1965); Giblin, 'Catalogue Nunz. di Fiandra', *ibid.* 9, 33 ff. (1966). The preponderance of the French-trained among the diocesan clergy just before the revolution may be seen from the figures presented to the government by Dr Andrew Dunne, secretary to the trustees of Maynooth from 1795 to 1803. He estimated that of a total of 478 students in the continental colleges 348 were in France, as against only sixteen in Rome. Of the remainder, seventy were in the Austrian Netherlands (Louvain and Antwerp), thirty-two in Spain (Salamanca) and twelve in Portugal (Lisbon) – three countries each with its own version of the 'Gallican' tradition (Healy, *Maynooth College*, 696).

such explanation of this tendency in Ireland must be treated
with considerable reserve. If we are to try to pinpoint the
source of such development, it would seem that we must
look, not to Jansenism, but to an influence from English
eighteenth-century spirituality which might be summed up
under the name of Richard Challoner.

There is general agreement that the chief formative
influence on Challoner's spirituality, after the Bible, was St
Francis de Sales. The experiences of his life in penal-day
London might be adduced as the explanation of the streak of
sadness verging on severity which might be considered a
characteristic of Challoner foreign to St Francis. This
contrast must not be pushed too far, however. 'He was very
cheerful,' said Charles Butler of Challoner in an often-quoted
judgement, 'and the cause of cheerfulness in others, but he
stopped very short of mirth.' There is indeed a strong
temptation to link the known popularity of Challoner's
works in Ireland of the penal times with the equal popularity
of the *Introduction to the Devout Life* by St Francis de Sales.
The list of eighteenth-century 'best-sellers' already given
includes also, it will be remembered, another author from
the great spiritual revival in France at the beginning of the
seventeenth century, *The Holy Court,* published by Nicholas
Caussin, a Jesuit, in 1624, before Jansenism had begun to
exert its influence.

No doubt any comparison between Irish penal-day
spirituality and the spirituality of Challoner and 'the school
of Challoner' in England cannot be made without serious
qualifications, and it certainly cannot be said that this
spirituality of 'the Challoner school' was the only influence
at work. It may be too that the relationship is more exactly
expressed as one of dependence on a common source rather
than of direct Irish dependence on the English school. We
must also, of course, ask the question, even if no really
precise answer is possible, as to the extent of this influence –
how far down did it penetrate? For the laity, it will be obvious
that considerable differences are to be expected between the
English-speaking urban middle-class on the one hand, and

the Irish-speaking section of the peasantry on the other. The influence on the latter must have been very slight indeed. But it need not be a cause for surprise that English and Irish spirituality should develop some common characteristics as a result of a shared experience of long oppression, or that a notable mark of that experience should be a severe and rigid, almost anxious morality. What does need to be said is that any attempt to find the source of this 'anxious morality' in Jansenism receives scant support from the facts of history as at present known. The nature of penal-day spirituality is of some importance, for it was at this time that the Irish Catholics formed the store of spiritual capital which has been their main sustenance down to very recent times.

III

IRISH EXILES IN CATHOLIC EUROPE

Cathaldus Giblin, O.F.M.

THE defeat of James II at the Boyne in July 1690, the violation of the treaty of Limerick and the subsequent persecution of Catholics forced thousands of Irish to seek refuge on the continent of Europe during the last decade of the seventeenth century. The exodus continued, though in a lesser degree, during the reigns of Anne (1702-14) and of George I (1714-27). The first half of the reign of George II saw little abatement in the migration abroad, but from 1745 onwards the numbers leaving Ireland because of persecution gradually diminished.

These fugitives included people from every walk of life: farmers, students, soldiers, merchants, priests and bishops. Boys and girls went abroad in search of an education denied them at home. Aspirants to the priesthood slipped away to do their studies at one of the Irish colleges in France, Spain or elsewhere. Young women anxious to embrace the religious life left home to test their vocations or take vows in foreign convents. Priests and religious sought shelter and peace amongst their fellow-countrymen in exile. Bishops, banished from their dioceses, took up temporary abode overseas until they found it opportune to return to their flocks. The Irish colleges served as havens of shelter for a great number of these exiles and afforded them accommodation until it was possible for them to return home.

Many of them, however, never again set foot on their native soil. No detailed records are extant concerning most of those who chose to stay abroad. This is especially true of the hundreds of Irish nuns who lie buried in the cemeteries of foreign convents where they passed hidden, secluded lives. A fair proportion of the priests ordained outside Ireland settled down in the land of their adoption and ministered as pastors, teachers, military and naval chaplains, or tutors to noble families. Some of the more fortunate acquired benefices which allowed them to live in reasonable comfort. Many had little or no desire to return home. Even a few of the bishops preferred to reside permanently abroad rather than face the hardships of life in an Irish diocese.

For a great part of the eighteenth century the hopes and aspirations of these Irish beyond the sea lay in the exiled members of the House of Stuart, James II and his son, the Old Pretender. These monarchs and the exiled Irish were companions in distress and their fortunes were inextricably entwined. With few exceptions the Irish abroad looked to the Stuarts for sympathy, succour and advancement. They were not disappointed. The Stuart court, first at St Germain and later at Rome, tried hard to relieve the sufferings and destitution of the banished Irish but found it impossible to meet the numerous demands on its generosity. Stuart resources were meagre in the extreme, but whenever there was money to distribute the Irish often received more than their due share of it; when the funds ran dry there was genuine sympathy in plenty. Whatever influence the Stuarts enjoyed was used repeatedly to interest cardinals, bishops, abbesses and lay potentates in the distressed condition of their Irish subjects. In this regard Mary of Modena, wife of James II, was outstanding. The fact that the Holy See acknowledged James and his son as rightful kings of Ireland and accorded them the privilege of nominating candidates for Irish sees drew the Stuarts and the exiled Irish still closer together and greatly enhanced the influence of these royal exiles in Irish church affairs. Only with the death of the Old

Pretender in 1766 did the Stuarts cease to play a significant part in the history of the Irish abroad.

THE COLLEGES

The most outstanding feature of the exiled Irish Church in Europe was the series of Irish colleges, almost all of which had been established before James II was compelled to abandon his kingdom. They numbered about thirty. Rome had three or four. In Spain there were five, at Alcalá, Madrid, Salamanca, Santiago and Seville. There were two at Lisbon. In France there were colleges at Paris, Nantes, Toulouse, Poitiers and Bordeaux. Apart from the three at Louvain, there were four others in the Low Countries, at Lille, Tournai, Antwerp and Douai. The Irish Franciscans had a large college at Prague in Bohemia and more modest foundations at Capranica in the province of Viterbo, Italy, and at Boulay in Lorraine. The Irish Capuchins had two at Bar-sur-Aube and Vassey in France: they had given up their foundation at Charleville in 1684. The church and priory of San Matteo in Merulana at Rome which had been granted to the Irish Augustinians by Pope Alexander VII in 1656 passed out of their possession in 1661; it was not until 1739 that an Irish community took up residence there again, when, at the request of James III, the Old Pretender, Pope Clement XII restored the building to the Irish friars.

Only two of these colleges were founded after 1690, that at Nantes for secular priests, and the other, at Boulay in Lorraine, for Franciscans. Of the two Nantes was by far the more important. During the first half of the seventeenth century a number of Irish priests and merchants had already settled there, but it was not until about 1690 that the priests came together to live in community. Between 1690 and 1695 they occupied a small building in the Rue de Chapeau Rouge which had been procured by two of their number, Ambrose Madden of Clonfert and Edward Flannery of

Waterford.[1] In 1694 when Aegidius de Beauvau, bishop of
Nantes, decided to suppress a community of Dominican
nuns in the city he handed over the vacated convent to the
Irish. An old, cramped building in the Rue Voltaire, it
served its purpose satisfactorily for a time, but as the number
of Irish seeking admittance to it increased it was found
necessary to erect a proper college. With the help of generous
donations from Irish Catholics at home and from local
Irish merchants a spacious new building was erected in the
years 1727 and 1728. When completed it had rooms for
some eighty students and four professors, a large refectory
with ten tables and spacious lecture halls. Throughout the
eighteenth century students were received there from all the
provinces in Ireland without distinction. In the early years
it catered for about forty students, but in 1765, when the
college was given the status of a seminary by royal letters
patent, it had sixty within its walls. Besides attending to
their studies, the priests in the college helped in the neighbouring parishes, acted as chaplains in hospitals and at the
port or gave instruction to the children of Irish merchants
in the city or its environs. In 1766, at the request of the
rector, Daniel O'Byrne, the seminary became a constituent
college of the university of Nantes and about the same time
the bishop of Nantes was authorized to devote in perpetuity
the income from the priory of St Crispin in Anjou to the
benefit of the Irish community. By 1778 the number of students was approximately ninety. They studied at home under
their own professors and those of them who so wished could
take degrees at the local university. At the French Revolution
the college ceased to exist. On 5 April 1793 the eighty
students and seven priests on the staff were imprisoned in the
Carmelite convent in the city, but were fortunate enough to
be released after a week and allowed to board a vessel in the

---

1. See Hurley, 'A bishop of Cork and the Irish at Nantes', in *Dublin Review*
110, 44-51, 351-62 (1892); Boyle, *The Irish College in Paris*, 122-4; Mathorez,
'Notes sur les prêtres irlandais réfugiés à Nantes aux XVIIe et XVIIIe
siècles', in *Revue d'hist. de l'église de France* 3, 167, 169-72 (1912): O'Boyle,
The Irish Colleges on the Continent, 192-200.

harbour which was setting sail for Cork. After Paris, the college at Nantes was the most important foundation of its kind in Europe during the eighteenth century.

In 1700 Leopold, duke of Lorraine, granted the Irish Franciscans permission to establish a community of ten religious at Boulay,[2] a town about fifteen miles east-north-east of Metz. Lord Taaffe, earl of Carlingford, who was Leopold's prime minister, played a notable part in procuring this foundation for the Irish friars. Bernardine Plunkett was the first guardian, and on 6 June 1700 he took possession of the old castle which had been placed at the disposal of the Irish community. A spacious friary of three storeys and a church were soon built on the site. The Irish soldiers stationed at Nancy and other Irish exiles as well as the people of Boulay contributed towards the erection and maintenance of the new foundation. During the eighteenth century the community usually numbered between twenty and thirty religious. In accordance with the regulation laid down by the bishop of Metz two-thirds of the priests in the community were required to have a working knowledge of German and the other third were to be similarly qualified in French so that they could attend to the spiritual needs of the people of Boulay and the surrounding districts. This regulation placed a severe strain on the friars. As well as doing pastoral work members of the community taught Latin and other subjects to boys in the locality. The friars had their own hopfield and vineyards and also cultivated the silkworm; brewing was first introduced into the district by them.

Shortly after its establishment novices were accepted at the friary. Courses were given in philosophy, moral theology and polemics to the younger members of the community and from 1730 onwards to outsiders as well. This foundation supplied many Franciscans to the Irish mission during the eighteenth century, but, as happened to most of the Irish

---

2. *Archiv. Hib.* 11, 118-53 (1944); Mooney, *Irish Franciscans and France*, 55-87.

colleges on the continent, the French Revolution and its aftermath put an end to its existence. The community was evicted in 1792. The last guardian, James Peter Connolly,[3] was arrested and imprisoned at Metz; although critically ill with tuberculosis, he was condemned to be deported in one of the prison ships, but he died on 4 August 1794 in the hospital at Rochefort.

Between 1735 and 1791 many Irish ecclesiastics found a temporary home at the seminary of St Nicolas du Chardonnet in Paris.[4] This institute, founded about 1628 by a priest named Adrian Bourdoise for the secular priests of the parish of St Nicolas who wished to live in community, was raised to the rank of a diocesan seminary in 1644 by the archbishop of Paris, and in 1710 there was added a house of residence for ecclesiastics from other dioceses. The official title of the institute was *La Petite Communauté de St Nicolas du Chardonnet*. The names of Irish priests and clerics figure prominently on the lists of its students from 1735 onwards. A few of these had been born in France of Irish parents and most of them had been ordained priests before entering the seminary. It would appear they paid their way by offering Mass for the intentions of the rector. Some of them had come to stay there while waiting for a vacancy in the Irish college, Paris, while others came to complete the course of studies which they had begun elsewhere. In all, fifty-four Irishmen studied at St Nicolas du Chardonnet between 1735 and 1791. Besides, many of the students at the Irish college, Paris, who had left Ireland before being ordained were given priestly orders in the church attached to the seminary. In common with similar institutions in France, St Nicolas du Chardonnet was suppressed in 1792. Ten of its priests were put to death.

Most of the Irish colleges overseas continued to flourish until the beginning of the French Revolution. The number of students in some of them was reasonably large; in others

3. Mooney, 'A Leitrim victim of the French revolution', in *Breifne* 2, no. 7, 332-52 (1964).
4. Boyle, 'Some Irish ecclesiastics at the seminary of St Nicolas du Chardonnet, Paris (A.D. 1735-1791)', in *I.E.R.* (series 4) 28, 480–91 (1910).

it was pitiably small.[5] The Irish college at Paris had the
greatest number and was the most important of the Irish
establishments abroad. In 1689 there were 180 students in
residence there; in 1739 the number had dropped to 90, but
by 1742 it had increased to 120. In 1776 it accommodated
160, of whom 100 were priests. In 1787, when the Irish
students at Paris had been divided into two separate communities, there were 100 priests at the Lombard College and
80 clerics residing in the Rue du Cheval Vert. Next in importance to Paris came Nantes, which in 1730 could accommodate at least 72 students; in 1765 it had 60 on its rolls, and
in 1778 the total number resident there was as high as 100.
When the revolution broke out in 1789 there were 70 clerics
and seven priests within its walls. At the other end of the
scale came Santiago where the number of students was
never more than six or seven; the number in the colleges at
Tournai and Toulouse never exceeded twelve. Strange to say,
the Irish college in Rome does not appear to have housed
more than thirteen students at any time during the eighteenth
century, and between 1772 and 1798 the number often fell
as low as three. In 1730 the college at Seville had only eight
or nine students, and by 1767 there were only four there.

Of the houses of study abroad under the direction of reli-
gious from Ireland, those in charge of the Franciscans at
Prague, Rome and Louvain, and of the Dominicans at
Louvain and Lisbon were the most important. During the

5. The numbers given here are drawn from a variety of sources of which the
following are the principal: A.V., Nunz. di Fiandra 153B, f. 31r; A.P.F.,
C.P., Visite 36, f. 721r; Burke, *Hibernia Dominicana*, 414-5, 428, 447-8;
Anon., 'The Irish College, Paris', in *I.E.R.* 2, 185 (1866); McDonald, 'Irish
colleges since the reformation', in *I.E.R.* 8, 472 (1871-2); Hurley, 'A bishop of
Cork and the Irish at Nantes', in *Dublin Review* 110, 46, 48 (1892); Boyle,
'Glimpses of Irish collegiate life in Paris in the seventeenth and eighteenth
centuries', in *I.E.R.* (series 4) 11, 438 (1902); Boyle, *The Irish College in Paris*,
52, 54, 122-4; Coleman, *The ancient Dominican foundations in Ireland*, 114;
Moran, *Spicil. Ossor.*, II, 283; O'Boyle, *The Irish colleges on the Continent*,
195; *Archiv. Hib.* 1, 123 (1912); 16, 3, 7, 81 (1951); 24, 110 (1961); 28, 78-84
(1966); Jennings, 'The Irish Franciscans in Prague', in *Studies* 28, 221-2
(1939); Mooney, 'A Leitrim victim . . .', in *Breifne* 2, no. 7, 337 (1964);
Fenning, 'The Irish Dominican province under appointed superiors (1698-
1721)', in *Archivum Fratrum Praedicatorum* 38, 301 (1968).

eighteenth century the average number in the community at Prague was about fifty; at times, however, as in 1742, it was as high as eighty, but by 1786 it had dropped to thirty-seven. Between 1756 and 1783 the college at Prague provided 115 priests for the Irish mission. The community of St Anthony's College, Louvain, usually numbered about fifty, while the houses at Capranica and Boulay had each about twenty. The number at St Isidore's College, Rome, varied between thirty and sixty. The Dominican priory of San Clemente at Rome usually had about twenty Irishmen. Before the disastrous earthquake of 1755 there were twenty-five in the Dominican community at Lisbon, all of them Irish. In 1707 the number in the Irish Dominican college at Louvain was thirty-eight; in 1742 this had dropped to twenty-four, but in 1767 it had increased to fifty. The total complement of priests and clerics in all the Irish colleges abroad about 1780 was approximately 600.

Any young man, whether ordained priest or not, wishing to leave Ireland to pursue his studies overseas had to contend with difficulties which, very often, could be surmounted only by good luck and a certain ingenuity on his part. He was breaking the law by going abroad for his education and it was for him to make use of every subterfuge to avoid detection by the many spies and government agents who made his journey so perilous, especially during the early decades of the eighteenth century. Consequently, he travelled in disguise and very often under an assumed name until he reached France or Spain or the Low Countries. A few resorted to exceptional tactics; for example, Patrick Joseph Plunkett in 1764[6] became articled to a merchant as an apprentice so that he could all the more easily evade the clutches of his pursuers. Some took ship at Cork or Dublin and sailed directly to France, while others made their way across England and sailed from London. It was not unusual for those who travelled by the latter route to do the journey across England on foot. Some, like Charles O'Donnell from

6. Cogan, *Meath*, III, 1.

Strabane, were more fortunate.[7] O'Donnell set out for the Irish college in Paris on 8 July 1777; it took him eighteen days to reach his destination. Having got as far as Drogheda, he took the stage coach to Dublin and from there the packet-boat to Liverpool which he reached at eight o'clock on the evening of 16 July. The following evening at five he left by the Liverpool fly and reached London at 8 p.m. on the nineteenth. Two days later he took an outside passage on the Dover coach, and eventually arrived in Paris on 26 July.

In the summer of 1731 Thomas Brouder, a Franciscan on his way to Prague, had to wait at Cork for three weeks and three days for a boat to take him to Le Havre which it took him eight days to reach.[8] He spent a night at the friary in Rouen and was fortunate enough to meet there another Irish friar who was returning to Ireland from Bohemia. Brouder exchanged his civilian dress for the habit worn by his confrère, who, as a result, was more suitably attired for slipping into Ireland unnoticed. When Peter Keenan, another Franciscan, left Ireland in the late summer of 1715 he had with him a large number of young men who were going abroad to pursue their studies.[9] On reaching the continent Keenan found that the Irish Franciscan colleges abroad were so full that none of them could accommodate the entire party. Accordingly he had to divide them into groups and let them make their way as best they could to Louvain, to Boulay in Lorraine, to Prague and to Capranica in Italy. That these Irish youths succeeded in reaching their various destinations safely shows what resourcefulness and ingenuity were necessary on their part.

Such journeys were costly even though most of the travelling was done on foot. Donations from relatives and friends at home helped to meet the cost in many instances, but in the case of those travelling to colleges under the direction of the secular clergy the expenses were sometimes covered by

7. Boyle, 'Glimpses of Irish collegiate life', in *I.E.R.* (series 4) 11, 435 (1902).
8. Burke, *Penal times,* 170-71.
9. Mooney, *Irish Franciscans and France,* 21-2.

G

burses which had been set up for the benefit of the students. The MacMahon burse[10] for instance, which was founded at the Irish college in Paris in 1710, allowed fifty *livres* to the holder to defray the expenses of his journey from Ireland to Paris; it was customary for the administrators of the burse to forward the required sum to Ireland, and a certain amount was guaranteed for the journey home. Priests returning from Spain received a grant for the expenses of their journey from the Spanish monarch.[11] The Dominicans had a procurator at Madrid who attended to the interests of his Irish confrères in this matter;[12] in the case of the Irish Franciscans the grant included sufficient money to enable them to purchase civilian attire for the journey.[13] The cathedral chapter of Seville was also in the habit of allowing Irish priests a certain sum to meet the cost of their journey home.[14] James III, the Old Pretender, purchased a house in Rome, the rent from which was devoted to defraying the expenses of priests returning to Ireland.[15]

Usually it pertained to the college to supply the daily needs of the student during his years of study there. In 1694 the superiors of the college at Lille[16] were satisfied if the new arrival had a sufficient supply of clothes for his first year as a student, and indeed they had dispensed with this regulation during the preceding four years. However, the Pastoral college at Louvain supplied only a room and food for the young man coming from Ireland; it was for himself to provide linen, books and other necessities.[17] Charles

---

10. Boyle, 'Glimpses of Irish collegiate life', in *I.E.R.* (series 4) 11, 434. (1902).

11. McDonald, 'Irish colleges since the reformation', in *I.E.R.* 9, 544 (1872-3); Fenning, 'The Irish Dominican province', in *Archivum Fratrum Praedicatorum* 38, 304-5 (1968).

12. Burke, *Hib. Dom.,* 183-4, 450. The Irish Dominicans at Louvain, however, often found it necessary to beg in public in order to procure sufficient money to meet the expenses of the journey to Ireland (cf. Fenning, *art. cit.,* 300).

13. A.V., Nunz. di Fiandra 153B, f. 31v.

14. *Archiv. Hib.* 24, 106 (1961).

15. O'Boyle, *Irish colleges,* 119.

16. A.P.F., C.P., Visite 36, 727r.

17. Moran, *Spicil. Ossor.,* II, 283–4; *Archiv. Hib.* 16, 31 (1951).

O'Donnell of the diocese of Derry has left us a list of the items he packed in his saddlebags before he set out on horseback in 1777 on the first stage of his journey to the Irish college in Paris:[18] nine shirts of fine linen marked C.D.; six ditto of a coarse kind, eight socks, nine pairs of stockings, two pairs of breeches, two flannel waistcoats, one French grammar, two Irish hymn-books, two pocket handkerchiefs, six pairs of ruffled sleeves. Certainly O'Donnell was not relying on the Irish college at Paris to supply him with clothes.

The money necessary to support the students at the colleges was derived from various sources. If the student happened to be a priest – and indeed this was frequently the case – he was able to contribute towards his support by saying Masses for the rector's intentions, and sometimes he received money for taking part in religious functions outside the college.

It was much more difficult for students who were not priests to meet their expenses. From the financial point of view such students might be divided into three classes. There were those who paid a pension to their college from private means or from money supplied by friends. There were others who held burses which covered at least their necessary expenses while they resided at the college. There was also a third class, those who were kept at the expense of the college itself. The first class were known as 'pensioners', and it was by this name Archbishop Carpenter referred to them when in February 1785 he sent two boys to the Irish college at Lisbon.[19] 'I ventured, however,' he wrote in a letter to Rev. Augustine Kirwan, 'to send a couple of boys there about a year and a half ago, but as pensioners, for I sent £100 with them for their support, which must be followed by more if the suits of law be not attended with success.' Dr Kearney, rector of the Irish college at Paris in 1788, was insistent that pensioners should 'pay a round sum all at once'. He considered that nothing less than sixty guineas should be accepted

18. Boyle, 'Glimpses of Irish collegiate life', in *I.E.R.* (series 4) 11, 435 (1902).

19. *Anal. Hib.* 14, 53-4 (1944).

for a boy who was beginning his philosophy, and eighty guineas for a boy beginning his *troisième*.[20]

Numerous burses for the education of students were founded by people in Ireland or by Irishmen of means on the continent. Some few were given by foreigners who had an interest in one or other of the colleges. The Irish Pastoral College at Louvain[21] had a relatively great number of burses at its disposal; at least eleven of them were founded between 1692 and 1783. Such funds, however, had various conditions attached to their allocation, and as a result it was frequently very difficult to find a suitably qualified candidate to whom the bursary could be legally given. During the eighteenth century the allocation of burses was a constant source of contention. In 1731 Vincenzo Montalto, the administrator of the nunciature at Brussels, declared there were volumes of complaints in the archives of the nunciature dealing with the allotment of burses in Flanders.[22] A few examples of the qualifying conditions will show how easily disputes could arise. Rev. Nicholas Bodkin, who died in 1747, founded a burse[23] at the Irish college, Tournai, in the first instance in favour of the children of his sisters and their descendants, and after them, to the benefit of the families of Skerret of Headford and Martin of Ross. On the extinction of the said parties the presentation to the burse was to revert to the warden of Galway, and no priest ordained in Ireland could enjoy its benefits. The allocation of this burse presented immense difficulties; it was still being availed of in 1791 when the warden of Galway was asked to present for the burse a child not older than ten or twelve years who had a slight knowledge of French. This particular case, while illustrating the complications which could and did arise in the allocation of burses, also shows the tender age at which some of the students were accepted in the colleges abroad. Another

20. Boyle, 'Glimpses of Irish collegiate life', in *I.E.R.* (series 4) 11, 440 (1902).
21. Bellesheim, *Geschichte*, III, 117.
22. A.V., Nunz. di Fiandra 127, f. 371r.
23. *Anal. Hib.* 14, 63, 124 (1944).

burse founded at Tournai by Eugene Brady, a canon of the cathedral church of Namur, when he made his will in February 1767, serves as an example of the inevitable contention to which the allocation of such funds gave rise.[24]

Very often the founder of a burse gave precise instructions as to how its recipient was to be treated at the college. The holders of the O'Keeffe burse at the Irish college, Paris, were to be provided with wholesome food, with meat and bread, and with wine or beer for drink; they were to be kept clean and warm, and were to be reasonably provided with clothes, stockings, shoes, hats, linen, books and paper, and in general with everything necessary for their sustenance and their studies.[25] It was laid down that those holding the Maher burse at the college in Poitiers were to be fed when in good health and in sickness, and were to be provided every year with clothes proper to their state; they were also to be supplied with linen, a hat, shoes, a candle, wood, clean laundry, and given the price of a haircut.[26]

As stated already, there was a third class of student who was provided for out of funds at the disposal of the superiors of a particular college. These, funds donated by benefactors, differed from the burses, for it was not prescribed that they be applied only to candidates from a particular diocese or family. Bishop Plunkett of Meath in a letter written in 1775 throws some light on the circumstances surrounding the allocation of such funds.[27] He states that in order to be eligible a student 'must be of an age not too advanced for *troisième*, that is fifteen, sixteen, or seventeen, or thereabout ... In this supposition he will be received gratis, as soon as he shall win a premium at the university. Should this happen the first year, he will have nothing at all to pay during the course of his studies'. It was customary for Dr Kelly, rector of the

24. See Cunningham, 'The will and foundation of Rev. Eugene Brady, 1767', in *Breifne* 2, no. 8, 460-66 (1965).

25. Boyle, 'Glimpses of Irish collegiate life', in *I.E.R.* (series 4) 11, 439–40 (1902).

26. *Ibid.*, 440.

27. Cogan, *Meath*, III, 7.

Irish college, Paris, to admit such a student to the college at the rate of £10 a year until he succeeded in winning a prize, after which he had nothing to pay.[28]

The financial difficulties encountered by some Irish secular priests who were still studying were alleviated by money accruing to them from chaplaincies. Priests from the diocese of Dublin appear to have been well provided for in this regard. There was a chaplaincy worth 292 *livres* a year at Douai for a priest nominated by the archbishop of Dublin, and through the generosity of a certain Colm Morgan chaplaincies were founded at Louvain in 1777 and 1778 for two priests from the same diocese; Morgan also made provision for a chaplaincy at Paris for a Dublin priest which was worth 400 *livres* annually.[29]

Considerable sums of money were required for the upkeep of the thirty Irish colleges abroad which had a total personnel of about 600. The rectors relied not only on the burses but on donations from generous benefactors among whom were many foreign princes, bishops, priests and laymen. The Congregation of Propaganda at Rome gave some financial aid, but it was meagre and sporadic. By far the greater proportion of the money needed was supplied by the Irish themselves. For example, at Bordeaux the Irish college[30] had an annual grant of £200 from the king of France; Thaddeus O'Mahony, a former rector, donated 5,200 *livres* by his will dated 29 May 1702; about the same time a French lawyer made a bequest of 8,000 *livres*, and the wife of the president of the parliament of Bordeaux gave 1,200. The addition of a new wing in 1743 and a further extension in 1776 placed a great strain on the resources of the college, with the result that the four Irish archbishops found it necessary to petition the queen of France, Marie Antoinette, to supplement the endowment of 1,700 *livres* granted by Queen Anne of

28. Boyle, 'Glimpses of Irish collegiate life', in *I.E.R.* (series 4) 11, 440 (1902).

29. *Rep. Novum* 1, no. 2, 490-1 (1956).

30. *Rep. Novum* 1, no. 2, 384 (1956); Boyle, 'The Irish college at Bordeaux, 1603-1794' in *I.E.R.* (series 4) 22, 128-9, 130-1 (1907).

Austria. The Irish college, Paris, was fortunate in having two outstanding benefactors among the French clergy,[31] William Bailly, titular abbot of Saint-Thierry near Rheims who, shortly before he died in 1692, left the college 12,000 *livres*, and Abbé de Vaubrun, professor of the Sorbonne, who, apart from taking an active interest in the college over a period of eighteen years, at the time of his death in November 1746 bequeathed 30,000 *livres* to the rector. The Irish friars at Prague[32] had generous benefactors in members of the O'Farrell, Kavanagh, O'Donnell, Kelly and Taaffe families in exile, and at the beginning of the eighteenth century their library greatly benefited by an endowment made by Count Wenceslaus Adalbert von Sternberg. About 1694 the Irish college at Tournai[33] was in receipt of an annual grant of 300 florins made by a former bishop of the diocese, Maximilian Villain. The Irish college, Rome, does not appear to have had endowments of any great value,[34] and this probably accounts for its small quota of students. The English and Scots colleges at Rome each had double the allowance from the Holy See that was given to the Irish college. Pope Clement XII, on learning of this, put the Irish establishment on a par with the other two by allocating to it fifty *scudi* monthly. However, Cardinal Aldrovandi was later to reduce this grant by half.[35]

Sometimes a college was reduced to such dire straits that the rector found it necessary to quest or to travel to Ireland or England in search of funds. In 1720 the Irish Dominican priests at Louvain were compelled to quest in November and December to clear part of the enormous debt with which their college was burdened.[36] Luke McKiernan, president of

31. Boyle, *The Irish college in Paris*, 12, 30, 33-4; Bellesheim, *Geschichte,* III, 110-11, 115.

32. McGrath, 'The Irish Franciscan library at Prague', in *Franciscan college annual 1951,* 30; Mooney, 'A Leitrim victim', in *Breifne* 2, no. 7, 338 (1964).

33. *Archiv. Hib.* 16, 5-6 (1951).

34. O'Boyle, *Irish colleges,* 119.

35. See A.V., Nunz. d'Inghilterra 30, ff. 285r-286v.

36. Coleman, *The ancient Dominican foundations in Ireland,* 113.

the college at Douai, visited Ireland and England in 1764 and 1776 in search of money, and Martin Glynn, rector of Bordeaux, spent some time at home in 1776 on a similar errand.[37] The endowments enjoyed by the Irish college at Lille were never sufficiently large to support its students;[38] it was only by seeking alms and by accepting stipends given at funerals that they managed to survive. On 24 April 1711 the mayor and council of Lille made an order forbidding anybody except students from the Irish college to carry corpses for burial; a certain remuneration was received for this work. At times the students also sought alms at church doors. In February 1723 they asked to be allowed to quest at the churches in Lille during Easter week in order to clear the debts on the college. The Irish students at Bordeaux[39] also had the privilege of carrying the dead to the cemeteries, and this practice continued among them as late as 1780. In a letter to the Irish bishops in 1774 Martin Glynn, the rector, pointed out that the custom led to abuses, as it was a source of distraction and interfered with studies.

Students in an Irish foundation abroad sometimes pursued their studies in the college itself, or lectures were attended at a neighbouring university or at a Jesuit house of studies. A student entering at the early age of sixteen or seventeen usually completed nine or ten years' study before returning to Ireland as a priest. If he were already ordained before beginning his course of studies, he could expect to complete it within five or six years. There were some colleges, such as that at Lille,[40] which catered only for young men studying the humanities, who were then sent elsewhere for philosophy and theology. Of the students who left Lille between 1690 and 1694 one continued his studies at Rome, one at Seville, five at Lisbon, two at Douai and two at Paris. At the Irish college, Antwerp, the clerics studied the humanities, the priests

---

37. Bellesheim, *Geschichte,* III, 229; Boyle, 'The Irish college at Bordeaux' in *I.E.R.* (series 4) 22, 140 (1907); *Rep. Novum* 1, no. 2, 383 (1956).

38. Boyle, *The Irish college in Paris,* 130.

39. Boyle, 'The Irish college at Bordeaux', in *I.E.R.* (series 4) 22, 134 (1907).

40. A.P.F., C.P., Visite 36, f. 727r; *Archiv. Hib.* 16, 13 (1951).

theology; lectures were taken at the Jesuit college in the city or at the episcopal seminary.[41] At Douai the students were usually priests; they attended the university where they followed a course in philosophy for two years, in theology for three, and then devoted a further year to the study of pastoral theology.[42]

The Irish college at Nantes was in a peculiar position.[43] It was subject to the university but was allowed to have its own professors, two for philosophy and two for theology, who were obliged to keep the university authorities informed about the progress of studies. No outsiders were allowed to attend classes in the college. In 1766 the university stipulated that the two professors of philosophy must have an M.A. degree and the two teaching theology a baccalaureate in that subject; besides, the professors of theology were expected to take the doctorate within three years of their appointment. It was also prescribed that the four Gallican Articles be taught in the college. The students at the Irish college, Paris, attended lectures at one of the many colleges attached to the university, but more especially at those of Montaigu, des Grassins, de Plessis, Navarre and Boncour.[44] In 1736 the archbishop of Armagh wished to prohibit all Irish students from going to Paris because of certain doctrines then current at the university,[45] but the other Irish bishops opposed him on the point and no change was made. At Tournai[46] only the humanities were taught, after which the students went to Louvain, Rome or some seminary in Spain for philosophy and theology. The students at Salamanca studied theology at the university; they usually came from Santiago where they

41. *Archiv. Hib.* 16, 16 (1951); 28, 80 (1966); A.P.F., C.P., Visite 36, f. 729v.

42. Boyle, *The Irish college in Paris,* 127.

43. Hurley, 'A bishop of Cork and the Irish at Nantes', in *Dublin Review* 110, 355-8 (1892).

44. Boyle, *op. cit.,* 40; *id.,* 'Glimpses of Irish collegiate life', in *I.E.R.* (series 4) 11, 441-5 (1902).

45. See A.V., Nunz. di Fiandra 132, ff. 163rv, 325rv; 153A, ff. 389r–390r, 396r, 397r.

46. *Archiv. Hib.* 16, 5-7 (1951).

had first studied arts, and sometimes philosophy.[47] Because of constant friction between these two Irish establishments, the Jesuit rector at Salamanca, John O'Brien, arranged in 1747 that his students should come directly from Ireland. Until their suppression in 1764 the Jesuits had charge of the Irish college at Seville, and the students attended lectures in philosophy and theology at the college of San Hermenegildo under Jesuit professors.[48] In 1769, however, the colleges of Santiago and Seville were incorporated with Salamanca, which accepted students from all the four provinces in Ireland.[49] Yet another Irish college, that of Alcalá, was incorporated with Salamanca in 1785. Disturbances were rife in this small college which catered solely for students from the northern part of Ireland.[50] In 1729 the Irish bishops, in an effort to put an end to further dissension, had decided to place the college under the Jesuits, as the method of appointing superiors was the reason for most of the dissatisfaction there. The objections to the bishops' decision were so strong, however, that it was thought better not to enforce it. In 1778, Charles III of Spain, in his letter confirming the appointment of Dr Bermingham as canonical visitor, ordered that no more students be received at Alcalá when the group then in residence had completed their studies and that the college be incorporated with Salamanca. In 1785 Dr Curtis went to Alcalá to enforce the incorporation, but he was stubbornly opposed by the students; the doors were locked against him and the mayor and the police had to be summoned to force a way in. In spite of this, the incorporation took place and all funds held by Alcalá were transferred to Salamanca.

Those entering the colleges run by the Irish regular clergy usually did so before ordination to the priesthood. Normally two years were devoted to the study of philosophy and three

---

47. *Archiv. Hib.* 4, 33 (1915).
48. McDonald, 'Irish colleges since the reformation', in *I.E.R.* 8, 307-8 (1871-2).
49. Cf. *I.E.R.* 11, 110 (1874-5).
50. *I.E.R.* 9, 545-7 (1872-3).

to theology. As a rule students took lectures in the college under their own professors. At St Anthony's College, Louvain, cases of conscience were propounded daily, practice in controversy took place on Sundays and holydays and each student had to preach two or three times yearly.[51] Irish Franciscans who were placed in Spanish friaries had to study for six years before being allowed to return to Ireland.[52] About 1742 the course of studies in the Franciscan and Dominican colleges abroad was extended by two years.[53]

Somewhat later a similar change was introduced into the seminaries which catered for the diocesan clergy. The Jesuit rector of Salamanca, John O'Brien, stated in a letter written about 1747 that his students could find time only to complete six tracts of dogmatic theology, and remarked that 'no matter how well they are studied they are a small capital for hearing confessions and preaching without tripping'.[54] In 1787 the Irish bishops were of much the same opinion. They considered that the theological course should be extended to four years at least so that priests returning to Ireland would be better equipped to counter attacks being made on the Catholic religion.[55] However, in a few of the colleges, after the three years' ordinary theological course, a further year was devoted to pastoral theology, and more talented students were allowed to remain on for two more years to take the licentiate.[56]

The methods of choosing superiors in the colleges varied greatly, and it is little wonder that the system practised in some places gave rise to considerable dissension. The colleges at Alcalá, Bordeaux, Toulouse and Seville suffered most in this respect. At Bordeaux the rector, whose appointment had to be confirmed by the archbishop, was chosen by the

51. A.P.F., C.P., Visite 16, ff. 738v-739r.
52. A.V., Nunz. di Fiandra 153B, f. 31v.
53. *Archiv. Hib.* 28, 87 (1966).
54. *Archiv. Hib.* 4, 41 (1915).
55. Moran, *Spicil. Ossor.,* III, 409.
56. See A.P.F., C.P., Visite 36, ff. 729v-730r; *Archiv. Hib.* 16, 16 (1951).

students, usually for a period of three years.[57] Most of the students there came from Munster, and in order to retain control of affairs it was customary for them to elect a Munsterman as superior. This created much dissatisfaction within the college, and in 1717 the archbishops of Armagh, Dublin and Tuam brought the matter to the notice of the archbishop of Bordeaux. From 1733 onwards the choice of the rector was left entirely in the hands of the latter. This put an end to the disputes.

It was usual also for the Irish students at Toulouse[58] to elect their superior, but in 1694 the local archbishop, Mgr de Colbert, in the interests of peace reserved the appointment to himself; he allowed those in the college to present a panel of three names from which he chose the rector. After 1725 the bishop of Nantes[59] had complete jurisdiction over the Irish students there. The local bishop had the final decision in the appointment of the rector of the Irish college at Antwerp.[60] At Seville the superiors were changed every year and the peace of the college suffered greatly as a result.[61]

Early in the eighteenth century efforts were made to unite the English, Irish and Scots colleges at Rome and to place them under one rector.[62] All three colleges had Jesuit superiors, and it was thought that if the three bodies of students were amalgamated and placed under the care of one rector it would make for easier and more economical administration. The Irish at home and abroad were vigorously opposed to this move. About 1704 a group of Irishmen on the continent who styled themselves 'nobility, gentry, officers, and souldiers now exilled' addressed a passionate appeal to

---

57. Boyle, 'The Irish college at Bordeaux', in *I.E.R.* (series 4) 22, 137-9 (1907).

58. Boyle, *The Irish college in Paris,* 120.

59. O'Boyle, *Irish colleges,* 192-5, 197.

60. Moran, *Spicil. Ossor.,* III, 408-9.

61. McDonald, 'Irish colleges since the reformation', in *I.E.R.* 8, 472 (1871-2).

62. See Curran, 'History of the Irish college Rome', in *New Ireland Review* (new series) 32, no. 2, 65-75 (April 1910); *H.M.C. Cal. Stuart papers,* I, 235; A.V., Albani 167, ff. 192r-193r.

Pope Clement XI deprecating any union of the Irish students with the English, and in January 1714, James III, the Old Pretender, asked Cardinal Imperiali to use his influence to block the union of the three colleges. A short time previously Mary of Modena, James's mother, had made a similar appeal. In the face of such opposition and particularly because of the deep-seated animosity between the Irish and English students, it was not found practicable to proceed with the project and it was accordingly dropped.

The rectors of the Irish college at Salamanca were chosen by the Irish hierarchy and confirmed in office by the king of Spain. On the expulsion of the Jesuits the college was placed under the administration of two vice-rectors, but in 1778 Dr Bermingham was chosen as superior and confirmed in his position by King Charles III. Dr Curtis, who later became archbishop of Armagh, succeeded in 1781 and held the post of rector for thirty-three years.[63]

The Irish college at Paris had a rather complicated system of government.[64] First of all in line of authority came the archbishop of Paris. Then came the major superiors, who were the chancellor of Notre Dame, the abbot of St Victor's, and that great benefactor of the college, the Abbé de Vaubrun. Next to these came the four provisors, one from each of the civil provinces of Ireland, who were chosen by the students. The election of the provisors sometimes led to disturbances and from 1737 on they were chosen by the archbishop of Paris.

Douai college was also subject to a board of provisors who chose the rector from a list of candidates presented by the superiors of the Irish college at Paris. At one time the provisors included the local bishop, the lieutenant-governor and the rectors of the Irish, English and Scots colleges at Douai.[65] The right of nominating the rector of the Irish college at Lille pertained to the Irish Capuchin community

63. McDonald, 'Irish colleges since the reformation', in *I.E.R.* 9, 138 (1872-3); *Rep. Novum* 1, no. 2, 404 (1956).

64. Boyle, *The Irish college in Paris*, 28-9, 32.

65. *Ibid.*, 127.

at Bar-sur-Aube. The affairs of this college were also administered by four provisors, two of whom were appointed by the bishop of Tournai and two by the civil authorities at Lille.[66] It is interesting to note that in 1764 the rector chosen by the Capuchins at Bar-sur-Aube was rejected by the provisors because he had not a sufficient knowledge of Irish. The appointment of a president for the Irish Pastoral College at Louvain appears to have been reserved to the Congregation of Propaganda at Rome, but sometimes the nuncio at Brussels was authorized to choose him. In 1721 it was not clear who had the right of appointment.[67]

The suppression of the Jesuits was a severe blow to the Irish colleges on the continent as many of these establishments had been under the direction of the society or associated with it in some way. Generally the Jesuit rectors were held in high regard by their Irish subjects. In 1729, for instance, when the Jesuits were meeting with strong opposition at Paris, members of the Irish college there rallied to their defence.[68] At the suppression, the Irish colleges at Rome, Poitiers, Tournai, Lisbon, Salamanca, Santiago and Seville were deprived of their Jesuit superiors. In some instances the suppression had even more drastic consequences. For instance, the Irish college at Lisbon[69] was confiscated in 1769 by Pombal on the pretext that it was a Jesuit establishment. Dr Carpenter, a former pupil of the college, was sent to remonstrate with Pombal but he had no success. In 1782, however, on Pombal's death, Fr Michael Brady succeeded in having the college restored to the Irish. Poitiers, also in charge of the Jesuits,[70] in consequence of their suppression had its funds transferred to Paris by an order dated 23 August 1774. In 1781 the superiors of the Irish college at the Rue du Cheval Vert in Paris petitioned the

66. Moran, *Spicil. Ossor.*, III, 275-6.
67. *Coll. Hib.* 5, 97-8, 103 (1962).
68. Boyle, *The Irish college in Paris,* 34-5.
69. McDonald, 'Irish colleges since the reformation', in *I.E.R.* 8, 311 (1871-2); *Rep. Novum* 1, no. 1, 171-2 (1955).
70. Boyle, *The Irish college in Paris,* 124-5.

French king that they be given possession of Poitiers to help them to liquidate their debts, but the university of Poitiers, which then claimed ownership of the college, opposed the petition. On the expulsion of the Jesuits from Seville,[71] the Irish college there was taken over by the civil authorities. At the time there were thirty-seven students in residence, only four of whom were Irishmen, and they went to Salamanca to continue their studies.

The widespread opposition to the Jesuits in Italy was responsible in some degree for their being deprived of the management of the Irish college at Rome. As far back as the end of the seventeenth century complaints had been made to the Holy See about their government of the college. In 1693 Cardinal Barbarigo made a visitation[72] there and in his report cast a certain amount of blame on the Jesuit superiors. Yet another visitation was carried out by Cardinal Imperiali in 1719, and he too found fault with the methods used in running the college. During the second half of the eighteenth century it was thought that too many of the Irish students at the college were joining the Jesuits, and Archbishop Fitzsimons of Dublin[73] in a letter of 28 March 1765 to the Congregation of Propaganda went so far as to say that he considered the college to be 'rather a Jesuit than a missionary seminary'. Partly because of this, but more particularly as a result of allegations made by the students concerning the maladministration of the college by the Jesuit rector, Fr Petrelli, an apostolic visitation was held by Cardinal Marefoschi, protector of Ireland.[74] The findings were not favourable to the Jesuits, and by a brief dated 18 September 1772 Clement XIV empowered the cardinal to dismiss them from the government of the college.[75] The

71. McDonald, 'Irish colleges since the reformation', in *I.E.R.* 8, 472-3 (1871-2).

72. Bellesheim, *Geschichte,* III, 227-8.

73. *Ibid.,* 228.

74. O'Boyle, *Irish colleges,* 120; *Anal. Hib.* 14, 11 (1944).

75. *Bullarium Pont. S. Cong. de Prop. Fide,* IV, 145-7; Bellesheim, *op. cit.,* III, 228.

following year he suppressed the Society of Jesus throughout the world. At the Irish college, Rome, an Italian secular priest succeeded as rector. It is interesting to note that in a letter dated 11 December 1773 Archbishop Carpenter of Dublin suggested to Cardinal Marefoschi that the funds of the suppressed Jesuits in Ireland be devoted to the needs of the Irish colleges abroad.[76] The cardinal agreed with the proposal and on 26 January 1774 requested the archbishop to forward £300 from the said funds for the use of the Irish college at Rome which he considered to be worse off than any of the other colleges. In 1798 the college was temporarily closed when Rome was invaded by the French.

By 1799 only three or four of the thirty Irish colleges on the continent were operating effectively. The suppression of the Jesuits, the amalgamation of a few of the smaller colleges in Spain with that of Salamanca, the radical reforms of Emperor Joseph II in 1786, the French invasion of Rome in 1798, and above all the wholesale confiscation of clerical establishments which followed in the wake of the French Revolution, all contributed, in varying degrees, to the elimination of the Irish colleges from the European scene.

Santiago and Seville were incorporated with Salamanca in 1769 and the same fate befell Alcalá in 1785.[77] By a decree of Joseph II dated 29 August 1786 the flourishing Irish Franciscan foundation at Prague was confiscated and in July 1793 was put up for sale.[78] The onward march of the revolutionary armies in France and in the Low Countries between 1790 and 1797 made it impossible for the Irish colleges there to survive. They were regarded as English establishments by the French, and so were freely pillaged. On the other hand, the English looked on them as French. Consequently, they were not allowed any share in the com-

---

76. *Rep. Novum* 1, no. 1, 164 (1955).

77. McDonald, 'Irish colleges since the reformation', in *I.E.R.* 8, 472-3 (1871-2); 9, 546 (1872-3). See also J. C. Bouzas, *El colegio de Irlandeses de Santiago de Compostela,* 20-21.

78. Jennings, 'The Irish Franciscans in Prague', in *Studies* 28, 221-2 (1939); Mooney, 'A Leitrim victim . . .', in *Breifne* 2, no. 7, 337-8 (1964).

pensations made available to the English colleges.[79] The
foundations held by the Irish Capuchins at Bar-sur-Aube
and at Vassey had to be abandoned in 1790.[80] The Irish
Friars Minor who had tried to weather the storm at Boulay
in Lorraine were finally evicted in September 1792.[81] In
1795 the Irish Pastoral College at Louvain and the Irish
Dominican foundation there were closed on the occupation
of Flanders by the French.[82] Two years earlier, in January
1793, the seals of the Republic were affixed to the doors of
St Anthony's College and all efforts to save it proved fruit-
less.[83] The confiscation spread to Rome in 1798 with the
entry of the French armies into that city. Almost immediately
the Irish college was closed and the church of the Irish
Augustinians and the greater part of their priory levelled to
the ground.[84] The communities of the Irish Franciscan
college of St Isidore and of the Dominican priory at San
Clemente were dispersed, but one or two of the friars succeeded in staying on in each place on the plea of attending
to the spiritual needs of the Italians who frequented the
adjoining churches.[85] In this way the buildings were saved
until the storm had passed.

Of the numerous Irish colleges which dotted the map of
Europe during most of the eighteenth century only those at
Madrid, Lisbon and Salamanca continued to function un-
disturbed as the century drew to its close. A small number
of the suppressed colleges were to be re-opened in the early
part of the nineteenth century to welcome students for the

---

79. Nolan, 'Irishmen in the French revolution', in *Dublin Review* (series 3) 23,
378 (1890).

80. *Lexicon Capuccinum,* 173, 1784.

81. Mooney, *Irish Franciscans and France,* 78.

82. Bellesheim, *Geschichte,* III, 230; Coleman, *The ancient Dominican
foundations in Ireland,* 114.

83. Jennings (ed.) *Louvain Papers 1606-1827.* 497 ff.; Mooney, 'St Anthony's
College, Louvain', in *Donegal Annual* 8, no. 1, 43 (1969).

84. Jennings, *op. cit.,* 525, 526; Cogan, *Meath,* III, 220, 234; *Rep. Novum* 1,
no. 2, 434 (1956).

85. Jennings, *op. cit.,* 523; Cogan, *op. cit.,* III, 234; *The humble memorial of
the Irish Franciscans of the convent of St Isidore in Rome,* 1.

H

Irish mission once more within their walls, but they were to cater for only a fraction of the hundreds who were housed in Irish establishments abroad before the outbreak of the French Revolution.

PASTORS AND SCHOLARS

During the eighteenth century a considerable number of Irish priests decided, on completion of their studies, not to return to their homeland. This was particularly true of those who had been trained in the Irish colleges in France. Bordeaux and the districts surrounding it, as well as Brittany, provided a permanent home for many of them. Their contact with the people during their college days had given them a fluent knowledge of French. Moreover, they had become accustomed to the French environment and preferred the refined comfort of French society to the trials and privations awaiting them at home. They found no difficulty in becoming naturalized French citizens.

Such priests were especially welcome in the Gironde where there was a grave shortage of clergy. Indeed, as early as 1685 priests from the Irish college at Bordeaux had, with royal permission, begun to exercise their ministry in the parishes of the Gironde and more especially around Medoc and the countryside of Buch and Born where the parishes were poor.[1] Besides caring for the local population they also attended to the spiritual needs of the families of Irish merchants and businessmen who had settled in those districts.

A glance at the succession of pastors in some of the parishes of the Gironde will show the continuous presence of numerous Irish clergy there.[2] For example, the parish of Boyentran had Irish pastors from 1696 to 1766, and that of St Cristoly for almost thirty years. Cornelius Scanlan was parish priest of Civrac from 1726 to 1776 and was suc-

1. See Walsh, 'Some records of the Irish college at Bordeaux', in *Archiv. Hib.* 15, 92-141 (1950).
2. This and following details are taken from *Archiv. Hib.* 15, 107-24 (1950).

ceeded by Nicholas Madgett of Kerry who also spent some time as chaplain at Angers to Count James Fanning. James Bourke was in charge of Cardan parish from 1723 until his death in 1749. Cornelius O'Cahan was parish priest of St André de Culzac from 1711 until 1732; he was then transferred to Gauriac where he laboured for a further twenty-five years. In 1748 thirty-nine Irish priests were ministering in the Gironde; by 1760 the number had dropped to eleven, but in 1767 it was fifteen.[3] Religious from Ireland were also engaged in pastoral work in France, especially in the early years of the eighteenth century. Patrick O'Hegarty, O.P., who died at St Malo in 1704, served for a time as curate in the parish of Trélou in the diocese of Soissons, while other Dominicans such as John O'Murregan, Peter O'Hennessy and Murtagh Deane acted as curates in other parts of the country. Peter Butler, O.P., spent some time as parish priest in the diocese of Poitou.[4]

Other Irish clergy in exile served as military or naval chaplains in France, Italy, Spain and elsewhere, or as chaplains to hospitals controlled by the civil authorities. On 15 June 1701 John Kelly was admitted as chaplain to the Spanish army but his faculties were restricted to the cavalry regiment of Joseph de Pinolosa.[5] Dominicans like Dominic Roche, Dominic Kent and Thomas MacNevin ministered to the soldiers of the Venetian, French and Spanish armies respectively.[6] Malachy Stanton, a Carmelite, and Thomas Dillon and Thomas Glasco, Dominicans, acted as chaplains to the Irish Guards at Parma between the years 1702 and 1734.[7] The Franciscans Francis Burke, Michael Nugent, Peter Mellaghlin and Paul Gormelly all died in the middle of the eighteenth century while serving with the French

3. *Ibid.*, 136.

4. O'Heyne, *The Irish Dominicans of the seventeenth century* (ed. Coleman), 11, 19, 77, 107, 119.

5. *Archiv. Hib.* 23, 158 (1960).

6. O'Heyne, *op. cit.,* 93, 105, 206, 207.

7. O'Sullivan, 'The "Wild Geese" Irish soldiers in Italy 1702-1733', in *Italian presence in Ireland*, 96-7.

navy.[8] During the Seven Years' War Arthur O'Leary, O.F.M.Cap., was chaplain to a prison camp and hospital at St Malo and ministered there until 1763.[9] Patrick Curtis who later became archbishop of Armagh had a varied military career; he first served in the Spanish army, then in the Royal Hospital of Marines at Cadiz, and finally as senior chaplain aboard the Spanish ship *St Ines* on which he figured in some memorable exploits in the year 1779.[10]

A number of these Irish priests on the continent, particularly in France, enjoyed a regular income from benefices of various kinds. Quite frequently these benefices were in the gift of local magnates, and Mary of Modena, wife of James II, was most energetic in promoting the interests of her Irish subjects in this regard. For instance, in 1697 Gerard Dowdall held two small benefices at Liège;[11] in 1717 Charles Maguire was dean of the collegiate church of St Peter at Lille;[12] in 1747 Thomas Lusk held a canonry at Cambrai;[13] in 1769 Hugh MacMahon, rector of the Irish college at Antwerp, became a canon in the collegiate church of St Peter at Turnhout.[14] Shortly before the Revolution Bernard O'Brien of Killaloe was canon at Bethune in the diocese of Arras, and for a time acted as chaplain to the duke of Artois, brother of King Louis XIV.[15] Others, too numerous to mention, held similar offices in dioceses and cathedrals abroad.

Occasionally, when the death of a fellow-Irishman is recorded or when reference is made to a gathering of Irish clergy, we get some idea of how numerous were those Irish priests on the continent in the eighteenth century and of how varied were their occupations. When Peter Burke of the

8. Mooney, *Irish Franciscans and France,* 111.

9. Hayes, *Biographical dictionary of Irishmen in France,* 238.

10. *I.E.R.* 9, 139 (1872-3).

11. Bellesheim, *Geschichte,* III, 38.

12. *Coll. Hib.* 5, 75 (1962).

13. *Archiv. Hib.* 14, 90 (1949).

14. Boyle, 'The Irish pastoral college at Antwerp', in *I.E.R.* (series 4) 27, 228-30 (1910).

15. Hayes, *Biographical dictionary,* 217.

diocese of Clonfert died in October 1724 a short biographical note concerning him was inserted in the register of the
church of St Similien.[16] He had been parish priest of St
Similien, doctor in theology, rector of Pau, chaplain at the
hospital of St Julien and superior of the community of Irish
priests at Nantes. A letter written by Dr Markey, rector of
the junior Irish college at Paris on 21 August 1780[17] gives a
fleeting glimpse of a group of Irish clergy who were domiciled
in France at that time. The letter is addressed to Bishop
Plunkett of Meath and informs him that 'Abbé Flood sets
off in a few days for Cambray, where he is to spend the
remaining part of the vacation with Canon Kennedy. The
President, Aherne, and Reilly from Brussels are to be one
of the party. Canon Butler of Lille has promised to pay me
a visit at Ivry. Abbé Collins of Trente-trois prayed me to
present you his sincerest respects . . .'.

We are indebted to John Kavanagh who studied at Nantes
and was ordained priest in Ireland in 1774 for colourful
pen-pictures of Irish priests he met during his travels.[18]
Kavanagh was chaplain to the family of the Marquis de
Lambilly, but was persuaded to enter the French naval
service by another Irish priest, Murtagh Somers, who was
chaplain to Count Menou, governor of Nantes. On 1
October 1782 Kavanagh called at Algeciras where he met
Laurence McKeon, a priest from Kells, co. Meath, who was
attached to the local hospital, and Michael O'Brien, a
chaplain on board a ship named *Bien-Aimé*. On 14 November
he reached Cadiz. While waiting on the quay there[19] he had
a lengthy conversation with a Carmelite friar from Galway
named Cummins, and within a few days he came upon
several other Irish priests; among them were Fr Quirke
from the diocese of Ossory; Fr Dillon, an Augustinian from

---

16. Hurley, 'A bishop of Cork and the Irish at Nantes', in *Dublin Review*
110, 351 (1892).

17. Boyle, *The Irish college in Paris,* 55.

18. See Hayes, 'An unpublished eighteenth century Franco-Irish manuscript',
in *Studies* 28, 475-84 (1939).

19. *Ibid.,* 481.

co. Mayo; Felix McCabe, who attended to the spiritual needs of some of the local gentry; Dr O'Kelly, O.S.A., of Galway and another Augustinian named Negan who was chaplain to the Ultonian regiment in the Spanish service.

In May 1784 Kavanagh was at Angers where he met priests named Doyle, Murphy, Garvey and Traynor. Not far away, at Amiens, was Richard Ferris of Kerry, vicar general and rector of the local college. It was only natural that Kavanagh's presence in Angers called for a celebration among the Irish there, and on 13 May a small group came together to entertain him. The event is thus recorded in his diary:[20]

> We had a great and plentiful dinner at Mr Murphy's lodgings, at which were present and not idle seven Irish priests, Captain Kavanagh from Borris, co. Carlow, son to Mr Simon Kavanagh, an officer of a salt office about four miles from Angers. After dinner we went to the Tennis Court, where we drank of Holland beer which was most excellent. We all supped where we dined, after which we drank down some round half-dozen of good Touraine and Burgundy wines . . .

When, in the course of his travels, Kavanagh visited the Irish college at Toulouse he was far from satisfied with the reception accorded him by the rector, Fr McCarthy, who was, apparently, more interested in books than in visitors.[21] The rector received Kavanagh in his study, which, in the latter's words, was 'crammed with old St Thomas, St Jerome, St Basil, and the works of all the rest of the Holy Fathers, some of which lay flat on the floor'. After a short time the rector was called away, and Kavanagh was left alone 'with 10,000 books'. This passing reference to McCarthy's library is a reminder that some Irish priests abroad took a deep interest in the study of the sacred sciences; indeed a fair number

20. *Ibid.*, 484.
21. *Ibid.*, 483.

became professors in celebrated centres of learning and
authors of distinction.

Michael Moore and Lucius Hooke, both secular priests
and natives of Dublin city, were men of remarkable erudi-
tion. Moore had been provost of Trinity College, Dublin,[22]
for a short time during the reign of James II, but a sermon
preached by him in Christ Church gave offence to the king
and he was obliged to retire to Paris. When James set up his
court at St Germain Moore moved to Rome, where he was
appointed censor of books and professor of philosophy and
Greek. Eventually he became rector of a newly-founded
college at Montefiascone. On the death of James II in 1701
Moore returned to Paris; it was on his advice that Louis XIV
established the college of Cambrai at Paris university. At
various times he held professorships at Paris in philosophy,
Greek and Hebrew and was eventually promoted president
of the college of Navarre and *rector magnificus* of the
university. Amongst his pupils were such celebrated scholars
as Boileau, Fleury, Fontenelle, Montesquieu and the
historian Rollin. Moore was the author of at least three
works in Latin, one of which dealt with the study of Greek
and Hebrew. He died on 22 August 1726 in the college of
Navarre.

Lucius Hooke made his priestly studies at the seminary of
St Nicolas du Chardonnet at Paris.[23] He took his doctor's
degree at the Sorbonne and became professor of theology
there, but he was later deprived of the chair because he
neglected to read a thesis at the defence of which he was to
preside. On being reinstated he exchanged the chair of
theology for that of Hebrew. In 1769 he was appointed
custodian of the Mazarin Library and held this position
until 1791 when he was dismissed because of his refusal to
take the oath to the Civil Constitution. His publications

22. Ware, *Writers,* ed. Harris, 288-91; Donnelly, 'The diocese of Dublin in
the eighteenth century', in *I.E.R.* (series 3) 9, 847, 1009-10 (1888); *Archiv.
Hib.* 5, 7-16 (1916).

23. Boyle, *The Irish college in Paris,* 49-50; Hurter, *Nomenclator litterarius,*
V, 294-6; Hayes, *Biographical dictionary,* 126-7.

include works in French and in Latin, one of which, *Religionis naturalis revelatae et catholicae principia in usum academiae juventutis*, ran into three editions between 1752 and 1754. The *Mémoires du Maréchal de Berwick* edited by Hooke and published at Paris in 1778 shows he was also keenly interested in history.

Another secular priest, Francis Martin of Galway,[24] who died at Bruges in 1722, had a brilliant but somewhat turbulent career at the university of Louvain where he held professorships in Greek and Sacred Scripture. About 1701 he was chosen one of the regents of the faculty of theology, and from 1705 to 1717 was lecturer at the Collège du Saint Esprit. In the latter year he was deposed by the university authorities because of his obstinacy and his passion for intrigue. For a period he was archiepiscopal examiner and censor of books in the diocese of Malines. A man with a deep biblical and classical knowledge, he published many works of which the more important were *Scutum Fidei* and *Motivum Juris*; the latter gave rise to serious controversy and was placed on the Index.

Francis Hearne of the diocese of Lismore also won a high reputation for himself at Louvain.[25] In 1776 he was appointed professor of syntax in the Collège de la Sainte Trinité and occupied the chair of rhetoric there between 1781 and 1793. In the latter year he was promoted to the chair for sacred eloquence. Hearne had the distinction of being exceptionally proficient in the Flemish language; in 1785 he was chosen by the Flemish students at the university as dean of the *Natio Flandriae*.

William Bermingham who was a student at the Irish college, Salamanca, in 1751, became professor of Greek at the university of Coimbra. His friend Michael Brady was

24. Spelman, 'The Irish in Belgium', in *I.E.R.* (series 3) 7, 1100-6 (1886); Hurter, *op. cit.,* IV, 1058-9; Jennings, 'Irish students in the university of Louvain', in *Measgra Mhichíl Uí Chléirigh*, 86.

25. *Waterford Arch. Soc. Jn.* 1, 236-8 (1894-5); *Measgra Mhichíl Uí Chléirigh,* 92. See also Edouard van Even, *De Ierlander Francis O'Hearn die in Belgie de Vlaamsche dichtkunst beoefende* (Ghent 1889).

offered a chair in the same subject by Pombal. These two scholars are often credited with the revival of the study of Greek in the Iberian peninsula.[26] About 1780 John Lanigan of Cashel distinguished himself as a professor at the university of Pavia. Before returning to Ireland in 1796 he had at various times lectured in Hebrew, ecclesiastical history, theology and Sacred Scripture; he was reputed to be amongst the foremost biblical scholars of his day.[27] Patrick Curtis held the chairs of philosophy and astronomy at the university of Salamanca about 1790.[28]

The colleges run by Irish religious also had their share of men who won distinction in the world of learning. John Brett, Edmund Burke, Michael Peter MacQuillan, Thomas Burke, Christopher O'Connell and Christopher French were the most prominent theologians and writers among the Dominicans.[29] Dominic Brullaghan, O.P., was author of a handbook for missioners entitled *De missione et missionariis*, of which there were two editions, the first printed at Louvain in 1736 and the second at Metz in 1745.[30] Anthony O'Rourke was the most outstanding author among the Franciscans;[31] he was a member of the province of the Immaculate Conception in Spain and wrote several works on theology and philosophy, some of which were not published until after his death which took place in 1745. Francis Devlin, a Scotistic scholar of merit, and Francis O'Mellaghlin, both professors at Prague, published many works of distinction; O'Mellaghlin taught for some time also in the cathedral seminary at

---

26. *I.E.R.* 8, 311-2 (1871-2); *Archiv. Hib.* 4, 35 (1915).

27. Bellesheim, *Geschichte,* III, 720-6; *D.N.B.,* XI, 576-8.

28. McDonald, 'Irish colleges since the reformation', in *I.E.R.* 9, 141 (1872-3).

29. See Ware, *Writers,* 295; Hurter, *Nom. litter.,* IV, 651, 965, 1028-9; Quétif-Échard, *Scriptores Ord. Praed.,* 188-9, 195-6, 666-8; Bellesheim, *Geschichte,* III, 717; Burke, *Hib. Dom.,* 552; O'Heyne, *The Irish Dominicans,* 152, 153.

30. Quétif-Échard, *op. cit.,* 827-8; Coleman, *The ancient Dominican foundations in Ireland,* 7.

31. See Lopez, 'Notas de bibliografia franciscana', in *Archivo Ibero-Americano* (segunda epoca) 2, no. 3, 455-62 (1942).

Imola.[32] Anthony Murphy and Anthony O'Brien, who were also on the staff of the Irish Franciscan college at Prague, wrote useful treatises on various aspects of theology.[33] Of the Irish Augustinian theologians abroad, Mark and James Forstall were the most distinguished; the former taught at Gratz in Austria and the latter at Heidenfeld in Germany.[34] Edward Creagh. S.J., occupied the chair of theology at the Madeleine university, Bordeaux, until the suppression of the Jesuits in 1762.[35] Another member of the Society of Jesus, Joseph Ignatius O'Halloran, was professor of theology and philosophy at the same university and also at La Rochelle; he returned to Ireland about 1773.[36]

James MacGeoghegan, a secular priest, John O'Heyne, O.P., and Francis Porter, O.F.M., were prominent in the field of history. On 6 October 1690 James II named Porter his official theologian and historian. Although Porter was the author of various theological works in the last decade of the seventeenth century, he is best remembered for his compendium of the history of Ireland which was published at Rome in 1690.[37] Of greater importance, however, was O'Heyne's history of the Irish Dominicans which appeared at Louvain in 1706.[38] Porter and O'Heyne wrote in Latin, but MacGeoghegan chose to write in French. His history of Ireland ran to three volumes, the first and second of which were published at Paris in 1758 and 1762 respectively and the third at Amsterdam in 1763.[39] The entire work was dedicated to the Irish Brigade serving in France.

Some other Irish scholars abroad preferred to write in

32. Ware, *op. cit.*, 286, 294.

33. Bellesheim, *op. cit.*, III, 713.

34. *Ibid.*

35. *Archiv. Hib.* 15, 108-9 (1950).

36. Hayes, *Biographical dictionary*, 233.

37. See Ceyssens, 'François Porter, franciscain irlandais à Rome (1632–1702)', in *Misc. Melchor de Pobladura*, I, 387–419; Ware, *op. cit.*, 262, 280.

38. Quétif-Échard, *Scriptores*, 259-60; Ware, *op. cit.*, 295–6.

39. Boyle, *The Irish college in Paris*, 48–9; Hayes, *Biographical dictionary*, 180–1.

French. Thomas Gould, a Corkman who did his early studies at the Irish college, Poitiers, was, after ordination, sent to Thouars in La Vendée where he preached so eloquently in French that Louis XIV granted him a pension and the abbacy of St Laon. Between 1720 and 1733 Gould published four works in French explaining the teaching of the Catholic Church, in which he displayed a great keenness of intellect and a deep knowledge of Scripture.[40] A work in French by M. E. Fennell, dean of Killaloe, caused quite a stir when it appeared at Paris in 1726.[41] Bernard Rothe, S.J., who was a professor at Poitiers for many years, wrote poetry in the French tongue; he was also a literary critic, and had a number of his writings published at Paris and Amsterdam between 1728 and 1731.[42] David Heneghan, a Corkman who had studied at the Irish college, Paris, and at the Sorbonne, was the author of several articles in the 1759 edition of Moreri's *Dictionnaire*; the contributions on such men as Keating, Lynch, Molyneau and Nary, as well as the long essay on Ireland, come from his pen.[43]

A few Irish priests domiciled in Paris during the first half of the eighteenth century devoted their energies to publishing books in their native language. Those Irish books which were printed at Antwerp, Louvain and Rome in the previous century were no longer available. In 1730 a secular priest named Conor Begley had a fount of Irish type cut at Paris.[44] He then invited Hugh MacCurtin, who had already published his *Elements of the Irish Language* at Louvain in 1728, to come to Paris, and enabled him to print his *Anglo-Irish Dictionary* there in 1732. Ten years later Andrew Donlevy succeeded in having his Irish-English catechism printed at the same place.[45] This is a bulky volume of 518 pages with

40. Bellesheim, *Geschichte*, III, 716; *I.E.R.* (series 4) 11, 209 (1902); Hayes, *op. cit.*, 108-9.

41. *I.E.R.* (series 4) 11, 209 (1902).

42. Hayes, *op. cit.*, 277-8.

43. Boyle, 'The Irish college in Paris', in *I.E.R.* (series 4) 11, 209-10 (1902).

44. Boyle, *art. cit.*, 202; Hayes, *op. cit.*, 12, 172-3.

45. Boyle, *art. cit.*, 202-5; Hayes, *op. cit.*, 71.

the Irish and English texts on opposite pages; it also contains a short treatise on the elements of the Irish language. The expenses of publication were defrayed by a wealthy French gentleman named Philip Joseph Perrotin who was on friendly terms with the Irish at Paris and keenly interested in the promotion of their native tongue. A donation made by him provided an annual income of 300 *livres*, part of which went to endowing a professorship in Irish and part to making prizes available for students of the Irish college who showed a proficiency in that language. Yet another portion was to be set aside for the printing of devotional works in Irish destined for priests returning to Ireland. Manus O'Rourke, parish priest of Branles, a village in the *département* of Seine-et-Marne, composed many poems in Irish on religious and patriotic themes between 1700 and 1743, and made several translations into Irish from Latin and English.[46] The Irish-English dictionary of John O'Brien, bishop of Cloyne and Ross, was printed at Paris in 1768, but the actual composition of the work was carried out by the author while caring for his flock in Ireland.[47]

BISHOPS IN EXILE

In the last decade of the seventeenth century and during the first half of the eighteenth many Irish bishops were to be found residing in the Low Countries, Spain and France and subsisting as best they could on slender incomes provided by the exiled Stuarts, by the Holy See, or by friendly bishops and princes abroad. A few lived in comparative comfort, but quite a number led a precarious existence and passed their days in poverty and distress. Most were willing to return home at the first available opportunity and minister to their

46. See Mooney, 'Manutiana', in *Celtica* 1, no. 1, 1-63 (1946).

47. Boyle, *art. cit.,* 205. See also Jones, 'The Congregation of Propaganda and the publication of Dr O'Brien's Irish dictionary', in *I.E.R.* (series 5) 77, 29-37 (1952).

flocks, but some had little or no desire to reside in the dioceses to which they had been appointed. These latter were taken to task on more than one occasion by the authorities at Rome and ordered to go back to Ireland. Two or three of them could not be persuaded to do so.

In February 1692 there were six members of the Irish hierarchy gathered around James II at St Germain:[1] Dominic Maguire, O.P., archbishop of Armagh; James Lynch, archbishop of Tuam; Dominic Burke, O.P., bishop of Elphin; John O'Molony, bishop of Limerick; Piers Creagh, bishop of Cork and Cloyne, and Gregory Fallon, bishop of Clonmacnois. About six years later, shortly before 7 July 1698, Bishop William Daton of Ossory, who also spent some time at St Germain following his banishment from Ireland, presented the nuncio at Paris with a list of bishops in which the place of residence of each one was noted.[2] Maguire of Armagh was still at St Germain with James II; the archbishop of Dublin, Piers Creagh, was at Strasbourg; Lynch of Tuam resided at the abbey of St Amand in the diocese of Tournai; Dominic Burke of Elphin was at Louvain; O'Molony of Limerick was at Issy near Paris; John Baptist Sleyne and Richard Piers, bishops of Cork and Waterford respectively, were thought to have gone to Spain.

The privations which some of these exiled prelates endured and their efforts to return to their dioceses are brought home to us by the two Dominican bishops of Elphin, Dominic Burke and Ambrose MacDermott. Burke laboured diligently in his see for twenty years before he was compelled to flee to Flanders on the defeat of James II by William of Orange.[3] He was intent on returning to Ireland at the earliest opportunity but was advised by the internuncio at Brussels not to travel without a safe conduct and this could not be procured. On 24 May 1697 he wrote to the cardinal prefect of Propaganda to explain his position: if he went to Ireland, his life

1. Burke, *Penal times,* 135-6.
2. Moran, *Spicil. Ossor.,* II, 336.
3. *Ibid.,* II, 315-21, 324-5, 366-7; Burke, *Hib. Dom.,* 498.

was at stake; if he stayed in Belgium he would die of want as the money sent to him by Propaganda was completely exhausted. In November 1701 he contacted Rome again; he was then eighty years of age and in dire need. To make matters worse, the Irish Dominican house at Louvain where he resided was falling to pieces and the community was desperately poor. In the circumstances Burke found it necessary to accept the hospitality of the Irish Franciscans at St Anthony's College where he died on 1 January 1704.

Ambrose MacDermott,[4] Burke's successor in Elphin, had lectured in theology at Rome for some years before he was appointed bishop on 31 March 1707. His consecration was kept as secret as possible so that he could all the more easily slip into Ireland unnoticed. Posing as an Italian and travelling under the assumed name of Filippo Gerardini, Mac-Dermott arrived in London early in 1708. Despite the precautions taken, he was captured and spent four months in prison before being set free through the intervention of the Venetian ambassador at London. Nothing daunted, he decided to try again with the aid of a passport from the imperial court. While waiting for the passport he retired to the Irish Dominican college at Louvain. His Dominican brethren, however, were too poor to support him, and on the invitation of the abbot of the Premonstratensian abbey of Tongerloo he took up residence there at the beginning of September 1708. The cardinal secretary of state advised MacDermott not to expose himself again to the danger of arrest in an attempt to reach his diocese as he felt it would be impossible to effect his release if he were captured a second time. The bishop, however, was not to be thwarted. On 19 June 1709 he proceeded to Rotterdam and set sail for Ireland a few months afterwards. The journey was a nightmare. Storms and attacks by French corsairs kept him thirty-four days on the high seas. In addition, he lost all his belongings.

4. Bellesheim, *Geschichte,* III, 51-3; A.V., Nunz. di Fiandra 150, f. 97r, 195, f. 226rv; *Coll. Hib.* 4, 98–9, 100, 101, 106, 107, 116, 122-3 (1961); Fenning, 'The Irish Dominican province', in *Archivum Fratrum Praedicatorum* 38, 309-10 (1968).

Nevertheless, he eventually landed in Ireland and governed his diocese for eight years before his death in 1717.

In contrast, another Irish prelate made his way from Bohemia to Ireland with reasonable facility. Before Francis O'Rourke, O.F.M., was chosen by Propaganda to fill the see of Killala in 1707 he had been private chaplain to Prince Eugene of Savoy.[5] It was considered wiser and safer for O'Rourke to travel to Ireland as a priest and be consecrated on his arrival. To facilitate the bishop-elect, Prince Eugene procured a letter of recommendation for him from the Emperor Leopold. This letter worked wonders. O'Rourke reached London without let or hindrance and was even granted an audience with Queen Anne who actually gave him permission to proceed to Ireland. He was consecrated in Newgate gaol on 24 August 1707 and ministered to the people of Killala until 1732 when persecution forced him to flee from his diocese for two years.

Some members of the royal houses of Europe as well as other important personages, both lay and ecclesiastical, used their good offices to make life on the continent more bearable for those exiled bishops. William Daton, bishop of Ossory, was invited by Louis de Tressan, bishop of Mans, to reside in his diocese.[6] There was no room in the episcopal palace for Daton, but the prior of the Benedictines at Couture arranged accommodation for him in a house which was in the outer cloister of the abbey. Daton took up residence there in March 1699. Moreover, the French clergy furnished him with an annual income of 12,000 francs and he received 1,000 francs yearly from the royal treasury. A considerable part of this income was regularly forwarded to Ireland for the needs of his diocese.

When John Baptist Sleyne, bishop of Cork, was deported to Portugal in 1703 the Irish Dominicans at Lisbon wel-

5. Bellesheim, *op. cit.,* III, 51; Donnelly, 'The diocese of Dublin in the eighteenth century', in *I.E.R.* (series 4) 11, 923 (1902); O'Connell, *Kilmore,* 142-6.

6. Moran, 'The bishops of Ossory from the Anglo-Norman invasion', in *Ossory Arch. Soc. Trans.* 2, 466 (1880 83).

comed him into their priory of Corpo Santo, and the nuncio there, as well as the king of Portugal and his sister, Catherine of Braganza, contributed generously towards his support.[7] Indeed Sleyne was not the only Irishman to receive help from James V of Portugal; this monarch was particularly bene-volent towards the Irish, and on 28 September 1709 Pope Clement XI directed that a special letter of gratitude be sent to the king in recognition of his great solicitude for them.[8] Piers Creagh, who was transferred from the bishopric of Cork to the see of Dublin on 9 March 1693, was fortunate enough to be accepted as auxiliary by Cardinal Wilhelm Egon von Fürstenberg, bishop of Strasbourg in Alsace, where he resided almost continuously from the time of his arrival on 4 July 1694 until his death on 20 July 1705.[9] For a time Creagh had rooms with the Jesuits in the episcopal seminary, and it is interesting to note that a niece of his, Catherine Creagh, resided with him for a while before her death in 1704. Louis XIV, at the instance of Mary of Modena, provided him with an annual pension of 1,500 *livres* from the resources of the Benedictine abbey of Marmoutier in the diocese of Strasbourg.

Apart from Creagh, a few other Irish bishops were allowed to officiate on the continent during the eighteenth century. It was a welcome source of income for them. Clement X by the brief *Credita nobis* of 10 July 1671[10] had forbidden Irish bishops to officiate outside Ireland even though a local bishop agreed to their doing so, but on 13 July 1691, on the application of Bishop O'Molony of Limerick, Innocent XII withdrew this prohibition. Certainly Bishops William Daton of Ossory, Richard Piers of Waterford, James Brady of

7. Bellesheim, *op. cit.,* III, 41–3; Moran, *Spicil. Ossor.,* II, 369-71. For documents concerning his deportation see Moran, 'The condition of the Catholics of Ireland one hundred years ago', in *Dublin Review* (series 3) 7, 157-60 (1882).

8. Burke, *Hib. Dom.,* 158.

9. Bellesheim, *op. cit.,* III, 14-5; Moran, *Spicil. Ossor.,* II, 372-3; *Rep. Novum* 1, no. 1, 120-2 (1955).

10. Bellesheim, *op. cit.,* III, 8; Brady, *Episcopal succession,* II, 356-8.

Ardagh, Cornelius O'Keeffe of Limerick and John O'Brien of Cloyne availed themselves of this privilege. Daton was permitted by Louis de Tressan, bishop of Mans, to give confirmation in several of the parishes of his diocese, and sometimes Daton even accompanied de Tressan on his canonical visitations.[11] In 1709, 1710 and 1712 Piers of Waterford acted as auxiliary to the archbishop of Sens.[12] When Cornelius O'Keeffe of Limerick was obliged to flee from his diocese in 1734 he betook himself to the diocese of Nantes in Brittany where he had been parish priest at St Similien for ten years before his consecration. During his short sojourn there he assisted the bishop of Nantes in his episcopal duties. On 19 June 1734 he ordained fifty candidates to the priesthood and carried out a similar function in his old parish of St Similien on 5 March 1735.[13] John O'Brien of Cloyne and Ross spent the years 1756 and 1757 at Bordeaux and performed at least two ordination ceremonies there, one in December 1756 and the other in March 1757.[14] According to the Register Book of St Gregory's College, Paris, Thomas Whittingham and Francis Parker received tonsure in the seminary chapel on 4 July 1759 from Bishop Brady of Ardagh by permission of the archbishop of Paris.[15]

The possession of benefices by some of these Irish bishops helped them to live in reasonable comfort. For example, some time before March 1706 Bishop Hugh MacMahon of Clogher was granted a canonry in the church of St Peter at Caslet in the diocese of Ypres.[16] Cornelius O'Keeffe of Limerick in 1734 acquired possession of a number of benefices in the parish of Machecoul in the diocese of

11. Moran, 'The bishops of Ossory', in *Ossory Arch. Soc. Trans.* 2, 466 (1880-3).

12. Brady, *op. cit.*, II, 74.

13. See Walsh, 'Irish exiles in Brittany', in *I.E.R.* (series 4) 4, 357-60 (1898); Begley, *Limerick*, 181-3, 193-5.

14. *Archiv. Hib.* 15, 135 (1950).

15. *Publications of the Catholic Record Society* 19, 146 (1917).

16. Bellesheim, *op. cit.*, III, 74; Moran, *Spicil. Ossor.*, II, 385-6.

Nantes,[17] and James O'Daly of Kilfenora enjoyed a substantial income from one of the most valuable benefices attached to the cathedral at Tournai.[18]

The peace, dignity and relative ease enjoyed by some Irish bishops abroad resulted in a natural reluctance to return home where hardships and privations awaited them. The sentiments expressed by Daniel O'Reilly, president of the Irish college at Antwerp, were quite understandable when, in September 1747, he learned he had been chosen to govern the see of Clogher. O'Reilly bluntly stated[19] that he would prefer a benefice worth 300 florins in the Low Countries to the pitiful living of a bishop in Ireland where there was nothing but poverty and persecution. The news of his promotion had upset him so much that he was confined to his room for fifteen days with a fever which kept him in bed most of that time. However, it should be said, to O'Reilly's credit, that he went to his diocese and faced the hardships that awaited him. But others were not so brave, and during the years following 1733 the nuncio at Brussels and the authorities at Rome were anxiously trying to persuade a small number of Irish bishops on the continent to return home and attend to their duties. Three were particularly at fault: James O'Daly, bishop of Kilfenora; Richard Piers, bishop of Waterford, and Ambrose O'Callaghan, O.F.M., bishop of Ferns.

O'Daly, when promoted to Kilfenora on 27 July 1726, held a canonry at Tournai.[20] It was agreed that should he be appointed bishop he would be allowed to retain this benefice. Within eight months of his election O'Daly applied for permission to absent himself from Tournai while still holding the canonry there. The Pope granted him an indult sanctioning this arrangement. However, the bishop of Tournai and his chapter would not accept the indult as they considered it

17. Walsh, *art. cit.*, 360.

18. A.V., Nunz. di Fiandra 153A, ff. 202v-203r.

19. *Archiv. Hib.* 14, 89-90 (1949).

20. A.V., Nunz. di Fiandra 129, ff. 242rv, 332r-333v (*Coll. Hib.* 9, 30-32); 153A, ff. 202v–203r.

to have been procured surreptitiously. They believed O'Daly
had not told the truth to the Holy See. In their opinion he
had no intention of returning to his diocese in Ireland; what
he wanted was to be free to live as he wished at Paris. The
chapter had no objection to granting O'Daly the fruits of the
canonry provided he returned home to attend to his flock.
This the bishop refused to do.

   This incident and the non-residence of a few other Irish
bishops compelled the nuncio in Flanders, Valenti-Gonzaga,
to send a report in July 1735 to Cardinal Firrao at Rome
concerning the whole question of absenteeism. He bitterly
complained[21] about those Irish bishops who remained outside their dioceses without serious reason. They had no
scruples about being absent from their sees and frequently
stated they did not intend to return home. In the nuncio's
opinion this was becoming a habit with some Irish prelates
and they were thus setting a very bad example for others. He
did not hesitate to name the bishops he had in mind. O'Daly
of Kilfenora was at Tournai and had no excuse for staying
there as he was vigorous and healthy. Richard Piers of
Waterford had been in France for many years; he claimed
he was too old to carry out his duties in Ireland, but the
nuncio did not consider that a sufficient excuse for not
returning to his diocese. As for Ambrose O'Callaghan, the
Franciscan bishop of Ferns, there was absolutely no reason
for his ceaseless travelling. Indeed, O'Callaghan had no
excuse for abandoning his diocese because, unlike other
Irish bishops, he was in receipt of an annual allowance from
the Pope.

   The nuncio also complained that apart altogether from
these three there were other Irish bishops who left Ireland
on the slightest pretext and showed no inclination to return.
If the poverty of their dioceses with its accompanying incon-
veniences was the pretext for being absent they should be
replaced by others who would be more willing to face the
hardships involved. The nuncio was convinced that if this

21. A.V., Nunz. di Fiandra 131, ff. 294r-296r (*Coll. Hib.* 9, 49-51).

abuse of absenteeism could not be speedily remedied, ecclesiastical discipline in Ireland would be undermined.

During the last three months of 1735 there was further correspondence between the nuncio at Brussels and Cardinal Firrao about the continued presence on the continent of Bishops O'Daly, Piers and O'Callaghan.[22] Valenti-Gonzaga was instructed to do his best to persuade them to return home, but he met with no success. O'Callaghan was on the move as usual, and in October 1735 had made his way to Rome. Firrao met him there[23] and succeeded in getting a promise from him that he would return home. Before issuing a definitive order to O'Daly and Piers, Valenti-Gonzaga wrote to find out what arrangements they had made for the government of their sees during their absence. In their replies they tried to defend themselves.[24] Piers pleaded that the enemies of the Catholic religion in Ireland had a price on his head, that he had made an attempt to return but was captured and only secured his freedom through the intervention of the imperial ambassador; he had appointed vicars to attend to the affairs of his diocese. O'Daly of Kilfenora had arranged with the bishop of Killaloe to substitute for him. He pleaded that the discomforts to be encountered in his diocese, the lack of a suitable residence, and his age, which was sixty years, justified his absence. Nevertheless, he declared he was willing to return to Ireland as soon as his health improved, provided he were given sufficient money for the journey and an annual pension.

The members of the Congregation of Propaganda considered the reasons advanced by Piers and O'Daly and the comments on them sent by the nuncio. They decided to take a firm stand. On 27 February 1736 the secretary of the Congregation was directed to advise the two bishops[25] to petition the Holy See for coadjutors to whom they were to

22. A.V., Nunz di Fiandra 131, ff. 391r–392v (*Coll. Hib.* 9, 52); 153A, f. 347rv.
23. A.V., Nunz. di Fiandra 153A, f. 353r.
24. See A.V., Nunz. di Fiandra 131, ff. 453r, 490rv, 494r (*Coll. Hib.* 9, 55-6.)
25. Bellesheim, *Geschichte,* III, 107; A.V., Nunz. di Fiandra 132, f. 123rv (*Coll. Hib.* 9, 58-9); 153A, ff. 370v-371r.

cede any income accruing from their dioceses. Moreover, the nuncio at Brussels was instructed to inform Piers and O'Daly that even if they refused to apply for coadjutors, the Pope would proceed to appoint them. Before the end of April 1736 both prelates informed the Holy See that they agreed to accept coadjutors on the conditions laid down.[26]

In 1740 O'Daly was still residing at Tournai, and O'Callaghan, bishop of Ferns, though spending some time in his diocese, was visiting Rome almost every year.[27] It was reported in 1738 that Sylvester Lloyd, O.F.M., bishop of Killaloe, had not spent one month in his diocese during the previous five years and that he had toured England, Flanders, France and Germany several times in search of money and pensions.[28] Christopher Butler, archbishop of Cashel, resided in Ireland but lived mostly with his brothers in Lismore and Ossory, places outside his diocese. The bishops of Kilmore, Kildare and Meath were in the habit of spending most of their time in Dublin. Once again, on 12 August 1741, Propaganda directed the nuncio at Brussels[29] to inform those Irish bishops who were physically unfit to attend to their episcopal duties or who were not content to reside in their dioceses that they should apply immediately for coadjutors. Should they decline to do this, they would be given coadjutors whether they liked it or not.

Five years passed, but only a slight improvement had taken place. On 1 August 1746 Benedict XIV found it necessary to address a brief to the Irish hierarchy on the

26. A.V., Nunz. di Fiandra 153A, ff. 372v, 377r.

27. Bellesheim, *op. cit.,* III, 108; Killiney MS C 328: Wexford friary account book. O'Callaghan's visits to Rome may have been connected with a lawsuit he had with the Congregation of the Council (See *Archiv. Hib.* 28, 60, 73-4 (1966)).

28. Bellesheim, *op. cit.,* III, 108; *Archiv. Hib.* 28, 72-3 (1966). In justice to Lloyd, however, it must be said that he was absent from Ireland in search of a cure for a disease of the eyes with which he was stricken when ministering in his diocese in 1731; the nuncio at Brussels held him in the highest regard (See A.V., Nunz. di Fiandra 127, ff. 494r, 495rv, 131, f. 339r, 132, f. 263r: *Coll. Hib.* 9, 24-5, 52, 61-2).

29. A.V., Nunz. di Fiandra 153B, f. 27rv.

subject of residence.[30] He declared that it was 'a source of
no small affliction to him to find, that among the bishops of
Ireland, some are so forgetful of the cure of souls entrusted
to their charge, that one, from the moment he undertakes the
episcopal office, never resides in his diocese; another, after
having devoted scarcely a month to the concerns of his flock,
retires into England, and from thence to France, Belgium
and Germany; while some are accustomed to visit their
church only once in the year, and that merely for a few days,
as if it were for the purpose of relaxation'. The Pope ad-
monished the prelates in a fatherly way, and concluded his
remarks by enjoining on those who had become unequal to
the task of discharging the obligations of their office by
reason of old age or infirmity to petition him for coadjutors.
In 1751, however, the residence problem was still causing
concern at Rome. In that year the archbishops of Ireland
were instructed by Propaganda[31] to exhort their suffragans
to reside in their dioceses. Any bishop found to be remiss in
fulfilling this obligation should be reported to the Congregation so that suitable measures could be taken to remedy the
situation.

During the second half of the eighteenth century it was
rare to find an Irish bishop resident on the continent. John
O'Brien, who was promoted to the united sees of Cloyne
and Ross in 1748, paid extended visits to the south of France.
The last three years of his life appear to have been spent at
Lyons where he died on 13 March 1769.[32] James Bernard
Dunne of Ossory retired to Paris in 1757 and died there on
30 April 1758.[33] James Brady of Ardagh spent some time at
Paris in 1759.[34] The repeated admonitions of the Holy See
eventually bore fruit and improved conditions at home made
it less necessary for Irish bishops to seek refuge abroad.

30. Burke, *Supplem. Hib. Dom.,* 830-1; Brenan, *Ecclesiastical history of
Ireland,* 557-60.
31. Renehan, *Collections,* I, 468.   32. *Archiv. Hib.* 15, 135 (1950).
33. Moran, 'The bishops of Ossory', in *Ossory Arch. Soc. Trans.* 2, 504
(1880–83).
34. *Publications of the Catholic Record Society* 19, 146 (1917).

STUART NOMINATION OF IRISH BISHOPS

Almost all the bishops appointed to Irish sees between 1687 and 1765 were chosen on the nomination of James II or of his son, the Old Pretender.[1] Even before James II left Ireland to take up residence at St Germain he had been granted the privilege of nomination by Pope Innocent XI. He first exercised the right on 19 March 1687 when he named Gregory Fallon for Clonmacnois. Fallon was promoted fourteen months afterwards.[2] Only two other nominations were made by James before he withdrew to St Germain; on 8 June 1688 he requested that John O'Molony, bishop of Killaloe, be transferred to Limerick and Patrick Tyrrell, bishop of Clogher, to Meath.[3] Both were transferred in accordance with his wishes. This prerogative forged a bond of union between the Stuart kings in exile and the Irish Church at home and abroad during the eighteenth century and gave the Stuart court at St Germain, and later at Rome, an importance and an influence in Irish church affairs which were fully acknowledged by the Holy See and jealously guarded by the Stuarts themselves.

Not all the Irish clergy agreed that James II and James III should enjoy such a privilege. John O'Molony, bishop of Limerick, and a Carmelite friar named Joseph Power were the most outspoken of the small number who opposed it. O'Molony feared that James II might advance English clerics to episcopal rank in Ireland[4] and in this way extend and consolidate English influence throughout the country. Such was not the case, but O'Molony's fears were not completely unfounded. Power, a native of Loughrea, co. Galway, known in religion as Father Joseph of the Nativity, resided at Rome as agent for the Irish bishops at the be-

1. See Giblin, 'The Stuart nomination of Irish bishops, 1687-1765', in *I.E.R.* (series 5) 105, 35-47 (1966).

2. Ritzler-Sefrin, *Hierarchia Catholica*, V, 162.

3. Ritzler-Sefrin, *op. cit.*, V, 244, 263; A.V., Albani 168, f. 55r.

4. Lenihan, *Limerick*, 615-7; *Rep. Novum* 1, no. 1, 120 (1955); Bellesheim, *Geschichte*, III, 12-13.

ginning of the eighteenth century. He appears to have been
on very friendly terms with Pope Clement XI and on more
than one occasion pointed out to him that nomination by the
Stuarts placed Irish bishops in an invidious position.[5] Because of it they were considered loyal supporters of the Old
Pretender, and, consequently, were completely unacceptable
to the government at home. Power advised the Pope to
ignore the Stuarts when choosing bishops for Irish sees
because interference from that quarter only aggravated the
difficulties facing the Irish Church. 'These politicians at St
Germain,' he declared in a letter to the Pope on 18 December
1703,[6] 'have not gained one advantage for Ireland in the
temporal sphere during these many years, and yet they
pretend that they can satisfactorily guide the country in
spiritual matters too.'

Such complaints fell on deaf ears at Rome. Some doubts,
however, had been raised there in 1692 and 1693 as to
whether James II should be allowed to nominate candidates
though deprived of his throne,[7] but a rescript issued by
Innocent XII on 22 September 1693 made it clear that no
bishop would be promoted to a diocese in Ireland without
prior consultation with the exiled king. This assurance was,
on the whole, faithfully carried out. Between 1688 and 1
July 1697 no less than thirteen bishops were provided to
Irish dioceses. All had been nominated by James.[8]

On the death of James II in 1701 his son James Francis
Edward, then thirteen years of age, assumed the title of
James III and was immediately recognized by the Holy See
and by France as rightful king of England, Ireland and
Scotland. For some years the young monarch was under the
guardianship of his mother, Mary of Modena, and she with

5. See A.V., Albani 164, ff. 67r, 68r, 72v-73r, 74r, 76r-77r; Bellesheim, *op. cit.,*
III, 68-9.
6. A.V., Albani 164, f. 68r.
7. Brady, *Episcopal succession,* I, 339; Bellesheim, *op. cit.,* III, 12, 13;
Renehan, *Collections,* I, 298.
8. Ritzler-Sefrin, V, 147, 162, 172, 183, 188, 189, 200, 232, 244, 263, 299, 419.

the help of her advisers continued to nominate candidates for Irish sees. In 1704 Mary, in her son's name, proposed Thady Francis O'Rourke, O.F.M., for Killala, Ambrose O'Madden for Kilmacduagh and Denis Moriarty for Ardfert.[9] That Mary played a significant part in such nominations is borne out by a reply she made to James Lynch, archbishop of Tuam, who had written to her early in 1704 about a vacancy in the diocese of Elphin. In concluding her letter to Lynch she said:[10] 'When it shall be seasonable to proceed in the matter I will not fail to take your advice concerning the person most proper for the charge, and in the meantime I shall be glad if you sent me the names and qualifications of such as you think fittest to fill the see.'

In June 1706 James III reached his majority. A few months afterwards Cardinal Imperiali was appointed protector of Ireland at his request. In February 1707 he reminded the cardinal that the candidates nominated by his mother, Mary of Modena, in 1704 for Killala, Kilmacduagh and Ardfert had not been raised to the episcopacy.[11] Almost immediately Francis O'Rourke was appointed to Killala and Ambrose O'Madden to Kilmacduagh;[12] Denis Moriarty was not advanced to Ardfert because objections were raised against him by the clergy and gentry of Kerry.[13] All seven bishops promoted to Irish dioceses during the first eight months of 1707 were nominees of James.[14]

Between 1709 and 1713 James's right to nominate was being partially ignored by the authorities at Rome. His candidate, John Verdon, was appointed to Ferns in 1709 without his prior knowledge.[15] No attention was paid to his

9. *H.M.C. Cal. Stuart Papers*, I, 210.

10. *Ibid.*, 193.

11. *Ibid.*, 207, 210.

12. Ritzler-Sefrin, V, 79, 188.

13. See A.V., Albani 164, ff. 66rv, 69rv, 70r-71r, 122r-124v.

14. Ritzler-Sefrin, V, 67, 79, 162, 188, 189, 194, 263.

15. James nominated Verdon for Ferns on 16 June 1709 (*H.M.C. Cal. Stuart Papers*, I, 232), and although Verdon had been promoted to that see on 9 September 1709 (Ritzler-Sefrin, V, 200), James was still ignorant of the fact on 2 March 1711 (*H.M.C. Cal. Stuart Papers*, I, 239).

proposal that Ambrose O'Connor, O.P., be promoted to Ardagh.[16] Indeed, the Roman record of Christopher Butler's appointment to Cashel contained no reference to the royal nomination; neither did the briefs transferring Ambrose O'Madden from Kilmacduagh to Clonfert on 28 August 1711, and appointing Luke Fagan to Meath, Malachy Dulany to Ossory and Francis Burke to Tuam in September 1713.[17] James took umbrage at the slight being cast on him by the Holy See. When Cardinal de Noailles requested him in January 1713 to use his influence to procure Armagh for Patrick Plunkett, O.P., he bluntly refused to put forward Plunkett's name or the name of anyone else, on the plea that he was not then on good terms with the Pope.[18]

A letter dated 5 May 1714 from Cardinal Imperiali helped to restore friendly relations. It assured James that the Holy See had no intention of disregarding his right to nominate and a document from Clement XI confirmed this.[19] Rome had, however, decided that in future two briefs would be issued on the appointment of a bishop for an Irish see; one brief would go to James, the other to the newly-promoted bishop. To ensure that the Irish government would have no knowledge of the part played by James in the appointment, and to safeguard the bishop should his papers be captured, the brief given to the bishop would not mention the prelate's nomination by the Old Pretender. At first James accepted this arrangement, but then, on 12 July 1714, he declared he could not agree to it. As Rome was not to be deflected from its decision, James, on 24 May 1715, accepted the expedient of the two briefs,[20] and it would appear that this procedure

16. *H.M.C. Cal. Stuart Papers*, I, 232, 235, 239; Coleman, *The ancient Dominican foundations in Ireland*, 104.

17. Ritzler-Sefrin, V, 147, 162, 263, 299, 393.

18. Fenning, 'The Irish Dominican province', in *Archivum Fratrum Praedicatorum* 38, 333 (1968).

19. A.V., Nunz. d'Inghilterra 30, ff. 166r-167r; *H.M.C. Cal. Stuart Papers*, I 329-32.

20. *H.M.C. Cal. Stuart Papers*, I, 366.

was observed during the subsequent fifty years in appointing bishops to Irish dioceses.

Between 26 March 1718 and 1 September 1730 twenty-four bishops were promoted to sees in Ireland; each had been nominated by James III, and it is significant that in the great majority of these cases the appointment was made within a week or a fortnight from the date of nomination. All the fifty-five candidates raised to the episcopacy between 1731 and 1750 were also nominees of his.[21] Almost invariably the Holy See sought James's advice before an appointment was made, and at times it went so far as to set aside its own choice for the one proposed by him. Indeed, some bishops felt the Old Pretender had played the leading part in their promotion. For instance, shortly after Daniel O'Reilly was appointed to Clogher on 11 September 1747 he instructed Patrick Brullaghan, a Dominican at Rome, to inform James of how much he appreciated the great honour the king had conferred on him.[22].

Between 29 January 1751 and 24 November 1760 every one of the twenty-two bishops appointed to Irish dioceses had been nominated by the Old Pretender.[23] For some years before James's death on 1 January 1766 poor health prevented him from attending to affairs of state.[24] In consequence, it may have been his son, Henry Cardinal Stuart, who put forward the names of the four bishops who were chosen for Irish sees between 1760 and 1765. The last instance in which the Stuarts exercised their prerogative was in the case of Philip MacDavitt who was nominated for Derry on 21 December 1765.[25] Of the total of 129 bishops appointed to Irish dioceses between 1687 and 1765, all except five or six had been nominees of James II or his son, the Old Pretender. Prince Charles Edward was not recog-

21. Information compiled from Ritzler-Sefrin, V and VI.

22. *Archiv. Hib.* 14, 90 (1949).

23. Information compiled from Ritzler-Sefrin, VI.

24. See Vaughan, *The last of the royal Stuarts,* 98-101.

25. Ritzler-Sefrin, VI, 194.

nized as king on his father's death, nor was he granted any voice in the appointment of Irish bishops.

From 1766 onwards the choice of bishops for Ireland devolved on Propaganda. Recommendations and advice were accepted from Irish clergy and laymen at home and abroad in an effort to find the most suitable candidates.[26] As a rule preference was given to those proposed by members of the Irish hierarchy or by the clergy of the vacant diocese. The person chosen by the Congregation was then approved by the Pope and a brief of appointment was duly drawn up and despatched.

The fact that bishops were appointed to Irish sees so regularly in the eighteenth century is due in no small part to the exiled Stuarts. More than once James II and James III protested that they had always the good of the Irish Church at heart when choosing candidates. There is no reason to doubt this. The overwhelming majority of the bishops nominated by them proved to be upright men who were unswerving in their loyalty to the Holy See.

STUART BENEFACTIONS

From the time that James II and his consort Mary of Modena took up residence at St Germain, Catholic exiles from England, Ireland and Scotland looked on them as their chief support in facing the difficulties to be met with in a foreign land. Every new exodus from Ireland placed an added strain on the meagre resources of the exiled Stuarts, but despite their straitened circumstances James and Mary met the many demands made on them with sympathy and generosity. When they had no money to give they used their influence wherever they could to procure assistance and accommodation for the hundreds of Irish who appealed to them.

The arrival on the continent of great numbers of Irish

26. A.P.F., S.C., Irlanda 17, ff. 389r-390r, 709r.

regular clergy after the promulgation in 1698 of the law of banishment created a major problem for James and his queen. Many of those refugee religious were in utter destitution and at times dying from hunger. James and Mary were full of compassion for them. In a letter to Armand Jean, late abbot of La Trappe, on 15 March 1698, James, in referring to those Irish refugees wrote:[1] 'This puts a new burden on me, and I feel the torture of seeing them with my own eyes dying of want, after having shared with them what I needed for my own support.' Mary of Modena was no less sympathetic. On one occasion, when requesting prayers from a nun for those banished priests she remarked:[2] 'All the regular priests of the Irish mission, numbering about 700, have already been hunted out of that country. There are just now near 400 of them in France, and others are in Spain and Portugal, or in Flanders and Italy. I have seen several of them and they have touched me deeply.'

Much of the money distributed from St Germain came from the Holy See, but the Stuarts also gave liberally from their own private funds.[3] Between the month of August 1698 and the end of that year 27,364 *livres tournoises* which had been forwarded by the Holy See were distributed among needy Irish clergy,[4] including 211 Franciscans, 118 Dominicans, 26 Augustinians, 5 Canons Regular, 12 Capuchins, 5 Jesuits and 3 Discalced Carmelites. During the same period a similar amount, part of which came from collections made at Paris and Versailles and part from the private income of James and Mary, was also distributed by their majesties, and it is worth noting[5] that on this particular occasion the amount allotted to the Irish was almost four times as great as that given to the English and Scottish refugees combined. When the nuncio at Paris visited St Germain on 3 March 1699

1. Burke, *Penal times*, 132.
2. *Ibid.*
3. See, for instance, *H.M.C. Cal. Stuart Papers*, I, 135–6.
4. Moran, *Spicil. Ossor.*, II, 347–8.
5. *Ibid.*, 349.

James and Mary pointed out to him that further aid was necessary for the exiled Irish clergy and that civilian clothes had to be provided for eighteen priests at the Irish college, Paris, who were about to leave for Ireland in three groups of six.[6] As a result of their request the nuncio placed 6,000 *lire* at their disposal.

On numerous occasions Mary of Modena appealed in writing to cardinals, bishops, abbesses and others in positions of authority in her efforts to succour the exiled Irish. She was particularly diligent in assisting Irish nuns who turned to her for help. In 1695 Madame MacDonnell and Madame Mellifont were members of the community at the convent of St George at Rennes; both were Irish.[7] For some unknown reason, possibly lack of funds, the abbess decided that Madame Mellifont should move to some other convent. However, a letter from Mary of Modena on 8 August 1695 requested the abbess to retain Madame Mellifont at Rennes until she herself was in a position to provide help. Besides, Mary asked that Madame Mellifont receive the same treatment as Madame MacDonnell who had been accepted at the convent on the recommendation of the king of France. In the same year two Irish novices, Elizabeth and Margaret Luttrell, were experiencing difficulties about being professed in the Carmelite convent at Rennes.[8] In their distress they wrote to Queen Mary, who, in turn, requested the local bishop to take the matter up with the abbess. In 1697 an Irish girl named Wyer was able to continue her education at the convent of Notre Dame de Poitiers as a result of a gratuity provided by Mary.[9] Miss Wyer expressed a desire to become a nun, but she had no dowry. Queen Mary found a place for her in the abbey of Xaintes where the rule concerning dowries was not so stringent. Moreover, she sent a sister of the prospective nun to fill the place thus vacated at

6. *Ibid.,* 339-40.
7. *H.M.C. Cal. Stuart Papers,* I, 104-5.
8. *Ibid.,* 107.
9. *Ibid.,* 126-7.

Notre Dame de Poitiers and continued to pay the gratuity in her favour. Another young lady helped by Mary was Jeanne McCarthy,[10] three of whose brothers had been killed in the service of James II. Jeanne wished to become a nun in the Irish Dominican convent of Bom Successo near Lisbon. On at least two occasions Mary wrote to the master general of the Dominicans, Fr Antonine Cloche, in the girl's favour, and to make matters still easier for her James II, on 26 November 1699, certified that she belonged to a noble family.

Mary of Modena was scarcely less concerned about Irish priests and students in exile. On 30 June 1698 she recommended Fr Bermingham, the Augustinian provincial, and Fr Carroll, O.S.A., prior of Callan, to the prior of the Great Convent of the Augustinians at Paris; both had been banished from Ireland.[11] About the same time she besought Count Alessandro Caprara, auditor of the Roman Rota, to request the Pope to nominate Louis O'Neale, who was studying at Paris, to a vacant canonry in the collegiate church of Lille.[12] In 1699 she thanked the father general of the Feuillants for having placed several young Irishmen in the houses of his order at her request.[13] Through her intervention the archbishop of Bordeaux provided for the maintenance of eighteen Irish students.[14]

The death of James II in 1701 did not cause the slightest diminution in Mary's efforts to help the exiled Irish. If anything she felt she had an even greater responsibility towards them. A letter to Cardinal Sacripanti on 3 February 1705 congratulating him on his appointment as prefect of Propaganda[15] conveyed her fervent hope that he would have the interests of the Catholics in her son's three kingdoms at heart. James Francis Edward, her son, was still in his

10. *Ibid.,* 132, 144, 145.
11. *Ibid.,* 131.
12. *Ibid.,* 132.
13. *Ibid.,* 137.
14. *Ibid.,* 137-8.
15. *Ibid.,* 198-9.

minority. 'We hope,' she said in reference to her Catholic subjects, 'that they will feel the effects of your zeal, but particularly the Irish. . . .' Her vigilance and persistence in providing for the exiled Irish were truly remarkable. The father general of the Benedictines of the Congregation of St Maur had, at Mary's request, placed some Irish youths in various Benedictine houses and maintained them during their course of studies. In June 1702, when these young men were on the point of completing their education, she promptly recommended three other Irishmen to fill the vacancies.[16] Through her influence two Irish Franciscans were accepted at the *Grand Couvent* in Paris; in February 1703 when their course of studies was drawing to a close she proposed two other friars named Kerry and Dwyer to succeed them. Two years later Dwyer decided to leave the *Grand Couvent*. Mary, ever vigilant, wrote to Fr Frassen, the guardian, asking him to accept a young friar named Kennedy to take Dwyer's place.[17] For some years previous to 1704 the bishop of St Omer had provided for the maintenance and education of two Irish girls. When the places fell vacant about August of that year Mary immediately recommended two more girls, a Miss Creagh and a Miss Sarsfield. A year later she informed the bishop that Miss Creagh was about to enter the Irish Benedictine nuns at Ypres and requested him to allow Canon Creagh, the girl's uncle who held a canonry at Strasbourg, to conduct his niece to the convent.[18] Miss Creagh was professed at Ypres on 7 July 1710. Many more instances of Mary's tireless solicitude for the Irish could be cited.

IRISH NUNS

Every member of the Stuart family in exile showed a special affection for the Irish Benedictine nuns at Ypres.

16. *Ibid.*, 176.
17. *Ibid.*, 181, 199.
18. *Ibid.*, 195, 203.

The nuns, in turn, were loyal and outspoken supporters of the Stuart cause. The abbey at Ypres had been founded from Ghent in 1664, but not until 1682 could it be said to house the nucleus of an Irish community.[1] On 19 November of the latter year Dame Flavia Cary, a nun of English birth, was chosen as abbess and about the same time a small number of Irish nuns from other Benedictine communities in the Low Countries came to reside at Ypres:[2] Dame Mary Joseph Butler came from Pontoise, Dame Joseph O'Bryen from Dunkirk and Dame Ursula Butler from Ghent. On 29 August 1686 Mary Joseph Butler, the first Irish-born abbess, was elected.[3] By November 1687 the community numbered seven,[4] but within three years Abbess Butler was the only choir-nun in residence. She and four lay sisters lived in extreme poverty.[5]

Financial aid from various sources kept the abbey from extinction. During the years 1698 and 1699 James II made two grants of 1,000 *livres* each to the impoverished community from moneys sent to him by the Pope for distribution among Irish exiles.[6] An annual subsidy of 500 florins from the king of France, as well as donations from Mary of Modena, the bishop of Ypres and various Irish officers, also eased the situation.[7] Mary of Modena endeavoured to interest others in the welfare of the community and was so generous in her own benefactions that she has come to be regarded by some as the second foundress of the abbey. In early summer of 1700 Mary learned that Abbess Butler was on the point of death. With some trepidation she wrote to the bishop of Ypres and emphasized that the community might

1. See Nolan, *The Irish Dames of Ypres*, 13.

2. *Ibid.*, 53; Beck, 'The Irish abbey at Ypres', in *I.E.R.* (series 3) 12, 115-16 (1891).

3. Nolan, *op. cit.*, 78.

4. *Ibid.*, 199.

5. *Ibid.*, 208.

6. Moran, *Spicil. Ossor.*, II, 348, 351.

7. Nolan, *op. cit.*, 210, 222; Beck, *art. cit.*, 409.

K

cease to exist if the abbess died.[8] In order to save the convent
from extinction she proposed that four novices be received,
but the bishop would not grant this concession. Mary then
pleaded for permission to have two novices accepted. She
assured the bishop that the necessary dowries would be forth-
coming: 2,000 *livres* had been invested at Paris for this
purpose, and she herself undertook to donate 1,000 *livres*
annually until sufficient dowries for four novices were available. The abbess did not die for many years afterwards, but a
serious crisis had been averted and in 1702 full community
life was established.

According to the terms of the treaty of Utrecht the town of
Ypres, which had been ceded to the king of France in 1678,
was once again restored to Austria in 1713. This meant that
the Irish Benedictine nuns at Ypres were automatically
deprived of the annual pension which they received from the
king of France as well as donations which reached them from
the Irish officers and men in the French army in Flanders. In
1713 Captain James Surdeville of Dublin, who was then
resident at Rome, bequeathed them a certain amount of
money,[9] but by August 1714 the nuns were in such dire need
that they made a formal appeal for help to Pope Clement XI.[10]
At that time the community numbered thirteen, three of
whom were lay sisters.

Abbess Mary Butler died in 1723 and was succeeded by
Xaveria Arthur, whose term of office spanned a period of
twenty years. In 1718 their great benefactress, Mary of
Modena, breathed her last. By her will, made in 1712, she
bequeathed 3,000 *livres* to the Ypres community.[11] The
generosity of the Stuarts did not die with her. Her son,
James III, and his wife Clementina Sobieska whom he had
married in 1719, were staunch friends of the Irish nuns and

8. *H.M.C. Cal. Stuart Papers*, I, 149; Nolan, *op. cit.*, 216; Beck, *art. cit.*,
409-11.

9. *Anal. Hib.* 2, 48 (1931).

10. *Coll. Hib.* 5, 66-8 (1962).

11. A.V., Nunz. d'Inghilterra 25, f. 123r.

corresponded frequently with them.[12] On Clementina's death in 1734 James, the Old Pretender, continued to assist them. In 1740 he ordered that a sum of 500 *livres* be given to the abbess out of his own money, even though his circumstances 'were but very indifferent'.[13] In 1741 we find Abbess Arthur thanking him for alms. Some years later, her successor, Abbess Mandeville, graciously acknowledged the receipt of 100 *scudi* from James,[14] and yet again, in December 1750, she thanked him for his 'repeated goodness and fatherly protection'.[15] Between 1750 and 1752 the community at Ypres was in such straitened circumstances that they considered leaving the town and settling somewhere in the dominions of the French king. However, on the advice of James III they decided not to move.[16]

Mary Bernard Dalton succeeded as abbess in 1760. Six years later James III died, and on 28 February 1766 Abbess Dalton sent a message of condolence to Charles, his son, addressing him King Charles III.[17] In doing so she protested the traditional loyalty of these nuns at Ypres to the exiled house of Stuart. The Holy See, however, was not of the abbess's way of thinking; it refused to recognize Charles as king. This decision must have saddened the community at Ypres, but, partly as a result of it, the long-standing friendship between the nuns and the Stuarts ceased. Before Abbess Dalton died loyalties had changed. In 1782 the duke of Gloucester, brother of King George III, and his wife and their two children were graciously received at the abbey by the Irish nuns.[18]

Scholastica Lynch was abbess during the upheaval which followed the French Revolution. The convent was invaded by French soldiers on 13 January 1793, but as a result of the

12. Nolan, *op. cit.*, 402.
13. Nolan, *op. cit.*, 260-61.
14. *Ibid.*, 421-2, 448.
15. *Ibid.*, 454.
16. *Ibid.*, 270.
17. *Ibid.*, 468-9.
18. *Ibid.*, 471, 479-80.

intervention of James O'Moran, a general on the Republican side, no damage was done.[19] The community and their abbey survived the aftermath of the Revolution. Between the years 1682 and 1791 the choir-nuns professed at Ypres numbered forty.[20]

Moneys sent to James II by the Pope in 1699 for distribution among Irish exiles included 500 *livres* which were given to Mr Ronchi, almoner to the queen, for 'the community of poor Irish girls at St Germain'.[21] It is more than likely that this was a religious community, but the order or congregation to which the girls belonged is not specified. When Mary of Modena made her will on 18 August 1712 she stipulated that if these young Irishwomen were still at St Germain at the time of her death, her son, James Francis Edward, was to give them 6,000 *livres* even though 'it should please God he were not then returned to his kingdom'.[22]

The Irish Dominican convent of Bom Successo on the outskirts of Lisbon which was founded in 1639 continued to flourish during the eighteenth century. It was decreed at the Dominican general chapter of 1706 that up to forty Irish women could be received into this community. The nuns who were natives of Portugal were not to infringe in any way on the rights of the Irish.[23] The confessor was always to be an Irish Dominican who could speak Irish, English and Portuguese.[24] At a later general chapter in 1725 it was confirmed that the convent was subject to the Irish provincial.[25] Although the choir of the convent was damaged in the great earthquake of 1755 the nuns escaped injury. The community consisted of thirty-nine nuns in 1760. Nineteen of these had been born in Ireland; of the remainder fifteen were

19. *Ibid.*, 287-9: Beck, 'The Irish abbey at Ypres', in *I.E.R.* (series 3) 12, 811 (1891).

20. Nolan, *op. cit.,* appendix E.

21. Moran, *Spicil. Ossor.,* II, 351.

22. A.V., Nunz. d'Inghilterra 25, f. 125r.

23. Burke, *Hib. Dom.,* 453.

24. *Ibid.,* 452.

25. *Ibid.*

Portuguese and three had been born abroad of Irish parents.
Mother Josepha Plunkett was prioress at the time.[26]

Apart from these few convents on the continent whose
communities were entirely or predominantly Irish, small
numbers of Irish nuns were to be found in various religious
houses of women, especially in France and the Low Countries; an occasional community included one lone Irish nun.
For example, about 1690 Mother Mary Baptist, a refugee
from the convent of Bethlehem near Athlone, was a member
of the Poor Clare community at Fougères in France.[27]
Mary Mansfield of co. Waterford made her profession as a
Benedictine nun in 1704 at the abbey of Our Lady of Consolation, Cambrai.[28] Sister Jeanne Shiel of the order of St
Francis and St Elizabeth died on 30 September 1718 in a
convent at Nantes.[29] Early in the eighteenth century Catherine
Rice of Limerick held important offices in the convent of the
Immaculate Conception of Mary at Paris.[30] About 1754 a
Dublin girl named Warren was a member of the community
in the abbey of St Austreberte at Montreuil in the diocese of
Amiens.[31] In 1770 almost all the higher offices in the Carmel-
ite convent of St Denis at Paris were held by Irishwomen.
The prioress was Mother Anne of St Alexis Creagh. She had
begun her religious life in the Carmel of Pontoise where she
held many posts of authority before she moved to St Denis
with Mother Dorothy of the Cross Dillon. Sister Julie de
Jésus MacMahon who entered St Denis at the age of fifteen
was a close friend of Madame Louise, daughter of King
Louis XV of France, who took the veil there in 1770.[32] When
Nano Nagle sought an Irish nun to take charge of the first
Ursulines who came to Cork in 1771, it was a member of the
Ursuline community at Dieppe named Margaret Kelly who

26. *Ibid.,* 452-3.
27. Mooney, *Irish Franciscans and France,* 106.
28. *Publications of the Catholic Record Society* 13, 60 (1913).
29. Mooney, *op. cit.,* 106.
30. *Publications of the Catholic Record Society* 8, 403 (1910).
31. Mooney, *op. cit.,* 21.
32. Concannon, *Irish nuns in the penal days,* 82-4; Cogan, *Meath,* III, 4-5.

came to her aid.[33] Mary Corcoran, daughter of Peter Corcoran of Dublin and Mary Carroll of co. Meath, made her profession at Liège in the convent of the English Canonesses of the Holy Sepulchre on 1 November 1777.[34] Other Irish girls too numerous to name individually passed their lives in the seclusion of continental convents.

The tendency of more than one member of the same family to enter the religious state abroad is perhaps best exemplified by the four Preston sisters, Elizabeth, Frances, Mary and Margaret, who left Gormanston on 3 September 1718 for the convent of the English Canonesses of St Augustine at the Rue des Fossés, Paris. On 17 December 1719 all four were given the habit of choir postulants. Frances and Mary persevered and were solemnly professed on 6 September 1728. Mary was appointed mistress of novices in 1748 and held that position until her death in 1788 at the age of eighty-five. Her sister Frances died two years later at eighty-eight. Elizabeth and Margaret had left Rue des Fossés, but in 1724 they joined the English Benedictine nuns at Pontoise in northern France. Margaret did not persevere and returned to Gormanston. A fifth sister, Anne, as well as two nieces, Elizabeth and Bridget, also became Benedictine nuns at Pontoise.[35]

Convents of English nuns in France and the Low Countries were particularly popular with Irish girls who wished to enter the religious state. Many entered the English Carmelites and English Benedictines at Pontoise, the English Dominicans and Benedictines at Brussels, the English Poor Clares at Gravelines, the abbey of Our Lady of Consolation of the English Benedictines at Cambrai, the English Canonesses of the Holy Sepulchre at Liège and the English 'Blue Nuns' at Paris.[36]

33. Walsh, *Nano Nagle and the Presentation sisters,* 79.

34. *Publications of the Catholic Record Society* 17, 21 (1915).

35. See O'Donnell, 'Some members of the Gormanston family on the continent in the eighteenth century', in *Franciscan college annual 1963,* 35-41.

36. Ample evidence of this can be found in volumes 8, 13, 14 and 17 of the *Publications of the Catholic Record Society.*

No records are available concerning most of the Irish-women in foreign convents during the eighteenth century. Even the names of the great majority have eluded us. They lived in seclusion, unknown to all but a few, and were eventually laid to rest in the peace of a convent cemetery. It can be truly said that they formed a hidden Ireland beyond the seas.

It is no exaggeration to say that the survival of the Catholic Church in Ireland is due in no small measure to the welcome accorded to Irish bishops, priests, nuns and students by the Catholic countries of Europe during the eighteenth century. Only for the shelter and facilities offered in Europe there would have been no outlet, no haven of refuge for clergy banished by the penal laws, no centre from which to replenish the supply of priests. Without the colleges on the continent, efforts on the part of the government to stamp out the Catholic faith in Ireland might well have been successful. These colleges served as supply-stations, providing clergy to lead, guide and instruct the people. Without them the education of aspirants to the priesthood, in itself a gigantic task, would, in the circumstances, have been an insurmountable difficulty. Attempts to educate clergy at home would, of necessity, leave their training both haphazard and incomplete. Such a clergy, themselves insufficiently instructed and separated as they would have been from the mainstreams of Catholic thought, could present distorted and defective versions of Catholic truth to the people, instead of beliefs based on solid doctrine. As it was, the priests trained abroad kept the faith pure and in line with the teaching and practice of the Roman Church.

The exiled Stuarts also played their part in keeping Ireland Catholic. It is true that the Irish at home may not have admired them with the same enthusiasm as those abroad. Besides, it cannot be denied that their influence in the appointment of bishops made the government doubly suspicious of every priest elevated to an Irish see. For all that, the Stuart intervention guaranteed a fairly steady succession of bishops in a great number of the Irish dioceses. They could have used their prerogative of nomination to impose English prelates on the Irish, and the consequences, political and spiritual, would undoubtedly have been disastrous. But they chose Irishmen who, in general, proved to be zealous for the welfare of their flocks. To that extent, Ireland owes much to the exiled Stuarts and to the episcopal candidates proposed by them.

It should also be emphasized that eighteenth-century Ireland benefited from her close contacts with Europe. Apart from their training, many of the returning clergy had distinguished themselves in foreign universities. Some of them had spent a period as tutors or chaplains with aristocratic families and even at continental courts. These men brought back with them a culture and a clerical decorum which enriched and ennobled Irish life and helped to smooth the asperities and coarseness naturally engendered in a dissatisfied and oppressed people. Besides, their learning and outlook ensured that Ireland was not ostracized from the mainstream of Catholic culture.

The presence abroad of so many Irish with the consequent interchange of letters and news, as well as the constant comings and goings of priests and students to and from the continent forged a bond of unity and affection between Ireland and Catholic countries like France, Spain and Italy. Places like Paris, Rome, Prague and Salamanca must have been household names in the remotest corners of the country. Even those who never left the homeland must have felt they were closely associated with the Catholic nations on the continent which were providing shelter, education and assistance for their kith and kin. Irish eyes and minds were focused on Europe in hope, affection and gratitude.

The upheaval caused by the French Revolution had a shattering effect upon Irish ecclesiastical contacts with the continent. In the eighteenth century more than half the Irish secular clergy were educated in France, about one-third of them at Paris. But the last decade of the century saw Irish priests and students hastily abandoning their colleges in France and elsewhere, and despondently making their way homewards. Fortunately the restrictions imposed by the penal laws had by then been eased. This enabled the Irish hierarchy to set up colleges at home for the training of priests. In 1795 St Patrick's College, Maynooth, was established to fill the void left by the closure of such colleges as Paris, Nantes and Rome. A few slender threads still bound the Irish Church to the continent, but the close association with Europe which proved such an asset during the eighteenth century was never fully restored.